THE BRAINSMART LEADER

THE BRAINSMART LEADER

Tony Buzan, Tony Dottino and Richard Israel

Gower

Published by
Gower Publishing Limited
Gower House
Croft Road
Aldershot
Hampshire GU11 3HR
England

Gower
Old Post Road
Brookfield
Vermont 05036
USA

Tony Buzan, Tony Dottino and Richard Israel have asserted their right under the Copyright, Designs and Patents Act 1988 to be identified as the authors of this work.

British Library Cataloguing in Publication Data
Buzan, Tony
  The brain smart leader
  1. Leadership 2. Executive ability
  I. Title II. Israel, Richard, 1942 – III. Dottino, Tony
  658.4′092

ISBN 0 566 07962 3

Library of Congress Cataloging-in-Publication Data
Buzan, Tony.
    The brainSmart leader / Tony Buzan, Richard Israel, and Tony Dottino.
      p.   cm.
    Includes index.
    ISBN 0–566–07962–3 (hardback)
    1. Leadership. 2. Organizational change. 3. Teams in the workplace. 4. Knowledge management. I. Israel, Richard, 1942–
II. Dottino, Tony. III. Title.
  HD57. 7. B89 1999
  658.4′092–dc21
                              98–37054
                                CIP

Phototypeset in Plantin Light by Intype London Ltd.
Printed in Great Britain by MPG Books, Bodmin.

CONTENTS

LIST OF FIGURES

PREFACE

The BrainSmart Leader has an important story to tell: a story that takes you through the most recent brain research and places it in the context of business today. It's not about theory, it's about real BrainSmart Leaders, and their everyday corporate lives. It's about documented, benchmarked case studies involving some of the world's most successful corporations. It's about saving money and time – and making people think.

BrainSmart Leaders are the corporate change agents for the modern world. They win respect, commitment, integrity and loyalty from their people. They cultivate and engage employee talents aligned and committed to their organization's vision. Most important, they improve their company's bottom line.

You will learn from this book how you can achieve all this yourself!

This is a significant work for us. It's taken us all our professional lives to understand, develop and refine, and is the result of countless hours spent with clients and associates around the world. The book contains contributions from people too numerous to mention, yet wonderful in their support and belief in our vision. We thank them all, with special thanks to two special people: Michael Dottino for his vision and perseverance in helping to make this book a reality, and Vanda North, our cheerleader, proofreader and BrainSmart Leader.

Most importantly, this book brings with it a new understanding: an understanding of the business brain in action in a world where Intellectual Capital provides the ultimate competitive advantage.

Tony Buzan
Tony Dottino
Richard Israel

OPENING QUIZ

To assess your existing strengths and weaknesses, complete the following quiz. Then calculate your scores and carry out the instructions given in the 'Analysis' section.

This diagnostic tool is designed to guide you to those chapters in the book that you may wish to work on first to accelerate your learning. However, to become a fully rounded BrainSmart Leader you will need to read all the chapters and complete all the exercises.

1. Do you believe you can learn to be more creative?   Yes/No

2. Do you believe your recall of information can exceed
   90 per cent?   Yes/No

3. Do you believe you can accomplish anything to which
   you reasonably set your mind?   Yes/No

4. Do you have a success formula for reaching your goals?   Yes/No

5. Do you enjoy learning more about your chosen field?   Yes/No

6. Do you seek out experts in your area of interest?   Yes/No

7. Do you accept responsibility for where your life is today?   Yes/No

8. Are you taking full advantage of the skills and creativity
   of your team members?   Yes/No

9. Are you encouraging people to take chances even at
   the risk of failure?   Yes/No

10. Are your team members enthusiastic, energetic and
    have fun at what they do?   Yes/No

11. Do people ask you for information about your field of expertise?   Yes/No

12. Do you have the necessary knowledge to justify being promoted?   Yes/No

13. Are you using computers to obtain information?   Yes/No

14. Do you have a method for organizing ideas so that you can access them easily?   Yes/No

15. Do you have a tool that allows you to improve your ability to store information?   Yes/No

16. Do you and your team have customer measurements that provide feedback?   Yes/No

17. Do you feel that your staff or team members are working towards a high performance culture?   Yes/No

18. Do your staff or team members view themselves as a catalyst to initiate change?   Yes/No

19. Do you have a clear picture of where you want to be two, five, and ten years from today?   Yes/No

20. Do you find that your values (what you believe in) and your efforts (what you do) are aligned?   Yes/No

21. Is there something you wish to achieve that is worth sacrificing comfort and convenience for?   Yes/No

22. Do you believe you are born with creativity?   Yes/No

23. Do you think that human intelligence is the number one competitive advantage?   Yes/No

24. Do you believe that intellectual capital is the main change agent in business today?   Yes/No

25. Can you name five of your cortical skills?   Yes/No

26. Do you spend time reinforcing others for good performance? Yes/No

27. Do you think having a vision helps you to achieve
    outstanding results?   Yes/No

28. Do you understand how colour helps improve your memory?   Yes/No

29. Do you have a mental process to organize your thoughts
    for recalling information?   Yes/No

30. Are you able to spontaneously link ideas together to
    create solutions to your problems?   Yes/No

31. Is there a difference between information and knowledge?   Yes/No

32. Do you believe that you can double your reading speed
    with the right information and practice?   Yes/No

33. Are you able to list work activities which are performed
    on a monthly basis?   Yes/No

34. Do you know in detail how your work affects the person
    who uses your product and/or service?   Yes/No

SCORING

Score two points for each question you answered 'Yes'.

ANALYSIS

Add up your scores for Questions 21, 22, 23, 24 and 25. If the total is less than 10, read Chapter 2, Intellectual Capital.

Add up your scores for Questions 1, 3, 7, 10 and 18. If the total is less than 10, read Chapter 3, Our Creative Brain.

Add up your scores for Questions 14, 15, 28, 29 and 30. If the total is less than 10, read Chapter 4, Mind Mapping®.

Add up your scores for Questions 4, 19, 20, 21 and 27. If the total is less than 10, read Chapter 5, The Power of the Vision.

Add up your scores for Questions 3, 4, 9, 19, 20 and 21. If the total is less than 12, read Chapter 6, TEFCAS™: The Success Formula.

Add up your scores for Questions 8, 9, 10, 17 and 26. If the total is less than 10, read Chapter 7, The BrainSmart Leader.

Add up your scores for questions 5, 7, 10, 17 and 18. If the total is less than 10, read Chapter 8, People Power.

Add up your scores for questions 6, 11, 12, 13 and 31. If the total is less than 10, read Chapter 9, Managing Information I.

Add up your scores for questions 2, 11, 12, 15 and 32. If the total is less than 10, read Chapter 10, Managing Information II.

Add up your scores for questions 8, 16, 22, 33 and 34. If the total is less than 10, read Chapter 11, Process Innovation Through Teams.

INTRODUCTION

This book draws on the results of recent research into the functioning of the human brain to develop Brain Principles and techniques which will help you become a BrainSmart Leader.

Although the approaches described will no doubt bring you benefits in your personal life, we concentrate here on applying this knowledge to the business world, setting out a practical, easy-to-implement programme designed to give you and your company a competitive edge, and explaining how to convert intellectual capital into increased profits.

We suggest that you skim through the book first, to gain an overview of the contents. You will notice that each chapter except Chapter 1 follows a similar format, to make it easier to assimilate the material.

At the beginning of each chapter from Chapter 2 onwards, you will find a set of questions designed to inspire you and challenge your thinking process. Then, as well as presenting relevant information and guidance, we profile people who are using – and thriving on – the ideas described. We end each chapter with a series of exercises to help you integrate the leadership profiles, case studies, Brain Principles, a Mind Map summary and other tools into your thinking process.

What is a BrainSmart Leader, and how do you become one?

BrainSmart Leaders know that people are the primary asset of any organization, and that harnessing the creative and innovative ability of their workforce will help their company break away from the pack and remain competitive in the new global economy.

We will show you how BrainSmart Leaders inspire their staff to discover their natural creativity, express creative ideas freely, and motivate themselves to draw on that creativity indefinitely. We will explain how they guide their workforce so that they feel valued and part of a team, and build upon the group's own synergy. We will also show you how they motivate team members who feel burnt out.

Our goal is to provoke you to think differently about your role as a leader. We want to help you explore new possibilities that will transform you into a catalyst for productive change. We want you to understand how to develop both your own creativity and intelligence and that of others within your organization.

In the course of our work, we identified questions which had rarely been asked and had never been answered to our satisfaction, questions such as:

- Why do so many companies struggle to use teams effectively? (See Chapter 6, 'TEFCAS: The Success Formula'.)
- Why have so many company change programmes (such as TQM, re-engineering) been so short-lived and not produced the expected results? (See Chapter 11, 'Process Innovation Through Teams'.)
- Why do companies which have been successful for many years suddenly fail? (See Chapter 5, 'The Power of the Vision'.)
- Why do some companies recover from major 'failures', while others spiral into decline? (See Chapter 8, 'People Power'.)
- In a world of information overload, how can companies process information more efficiently? (See Chapter 9, 'Managing Information I'.)
- What does a manager need to do to reform successfully in the modern world? (See Chapter 1, 'Rich Bannon, Success Story' and Epilogue: 'The Tony Angelo Story'.)

We put forward answers to these questions, as well as addressing other leadership topics which our work has brought to light. It is our intention to equip you with the mental technology you need to prosper: the ability to apply your creative brain more effectively. Our journey begins with Rich Bannon's success story – a BrainSmart Leader who lives and breathes every principle and technique found in this book.

1 RICH BANNON, SUCCESS STORY

We asked some corporate presidents and CEOs: 'What are today's business issues?' They replied: 'Maximize shareholder value', 'Expand market share', 'Improve performance culture', 'Become more customer-focused', 'Put in place a process where real work gets done', 'People, people, people', 'Better returns on our investment in people', 'Cut costs' and 'Innovation'.

We asked some human resource directors: 'What are your toughest challenges?' They replied: 'Attracting and retaining talent', 'Dealing with the loss of loyalty in the workforce', 'Creating learning communities', 'Obtaining commitment', 'Bringing workers into the business model', 'Creating a performance culture', 'Making people more responsible for results' and 'Building community through teams that work.'

We asked some employees: 'What do you want from a company?' They replied: 'Talk straight to us', 'Listen to us', 'Share the rewards', 'Stop the programme of the month and just walk the talk', 'Make our work worthwhile, give it some purpose', 'Build trust', 'Let us learn something new', 'Bring us to the forefront', 'We want a new deal' and 'Job security.'

Perhaps you can relate to some of the above statements. These are the issues of our time. We believe the answers can be found in one word: leadership. But leadership is not new. What *is* new is the type of leader now required: a leader who can take all the above issues and make them fit together. You may be thinking, 'That's easy to write. Is this just another book of theory, conjecture and pie-in-the-sky thinking?' No. This is a book about *real people* – in fact, *real leaders*: leaders who go out there and make it happen every day; leaders who are applying the latest brain research in their companies and achieving extraordinary results. That's what this book is all about.

We use the term 'BrainSmart Leaders' to describe those who apply Brain Principles to business issues. We would like to introduce you to our first BrainSmart Leader – Rich Bannon.

If you ask Rich Bannon why he is a proponent of the principles we discuss in this book, he has a simple answer: 'Because they work!'

Bannon is currently a Senior Vice President and Corporate Controller of

Entex Information Services. Entex is one of the largest PC workstation integration companies in the United States, managing more than 600 000 PCs for Fortune 1000 companies with revenue of $2.5 billion. But it was several years ago, when he was with IBM, that he began to apply Brain Principles in his daily work, and it was there that his work helped win his organization *CFO Magazine*'s Reach Award for the highest level of re-engineering savings in the United States.

In short, Bannon is one of America's top leaders, and he is an example of what can happen when the principles outlined in this book are put into practice:

> When I started using them, I started fixing problems. When the people working on my team began using them, they began identifying problems and fixing them. I got immediate, tangible, measurable results.

That last point was crucial, because the IBM management team that Bannon had to answer to at the time was highly sceptical:

> They weren't overly interested in using this stuff. I had to convince them to do it. I promised them that we would produce measurable results or we wouldn't do any more.

Bannon had just been put in charge of a new organization at IBM that had been created to centralize all the administrative accounting work throughout the company. He was responsible for more than 500 IBM staff and contractors:

> At the time, IBM was in a downsizing mode, so there was a good deal of stress and paralysis. People were averse to risk, and we weren't getting much done. To make things worse, I had more work than people to do it, creating a stress-filled environment that led to even more mistakes being made.

His first task, Bannon realized, was to teach people how to deal with change:

> I held a meeting with my top managers, and we started developing a set of goals and objectives for the organization, starting with a mission statement and a vision. We spent two days wrestling with that. One thing that kept coming up was that people needed more tools, and more training. There was too much work, and not enough hours in the day to get everything

done. In addition to improving how we did things, we needed to become better at prioritizing our work.

Setting goals, defining success, prioritizing – leaders who align their teams with a goal will be covered in Chapter 6, 'TEFCAS: The Success Formula'.

Bannon called in Tony Dottino, and together they developed a strategy. They met with the managers above Bannon in the organization, then the managers who reported to him, and then all the other employees.

Bannon's first step was getting the management team to buy into his vision. He received not only their commitment and support, but also their active participation.

Bannon and Dottino used a detailed questionnaire to identify which parts of each person's job were most important. They were trying to find out whether everyone in Bannon's organization was in alignment with the agreed mission statement. Not surprisingly, they weren't:

> Things were definitely not synchronized. We thought the ship was sailing in one direction, and discovered that many people were rowing it in another.

Earlier in the year, Bannon had asked managers and employees to examine their work processes in order to discover which could be downgraded or eliminated. The effort was only partially successful:

> We could identify things to go after, but eliminating or correcting them was extremely painful.

Bannon and Dottino created Process Innovation Through Teams (PITT) Workshops to explore ways to improve team performance by analysing work activities, improving communication and unleashing creativity (see Chapter 11). During the team workshops, Bannon built a shared vision of excellence. This vision was codified into a working statement:

Excellence Through Teamwork.

He asked each manager to share the vision with every person in their department and seek employee feedback, both positive and negative. The result of this exercise was that upper management, his management staff, and all staff members came to agreement on the central goal of the organization:

> Like any manager, I have all these ideas of what people working with me should be doing. But in truth I know that I never really understand what the issues are as well as the person directly involved with them. [We will discuss this in Chapter 7.]

We explained the benefits to Bannon's organization of using a team approach to Mind Mapping:

> I defined broad areas, like payroll and sub-activities below that, and let people aggressively challenge them, identify the problem areas and find ways to correct them. One of the first things they discovered was that in some cases they thought they were working on one problem, but after Mind Mapping and brainstorming, they realized that the real inhibitor to making progress was something else entirely. That is the value of using group Mind Maps and brainstorming with four or five people. [Mind Mapping is covered in Chapter 4.]

Bannon summarizes it well:

> If you take process analysis skills, an understanding of your customer and your supplier, add some creativity, and get people communicating and working in teams, it all ties together. That is the formula for success.

This wasn't an easy change, of course: 'People were paralysed in the beginning,' says Bannon. 'They were afraid of change. We needed to figure out a way of helping them.'

The master or victim of change?

Bannon told the workshop participants that they were all change agents, and that the tools they were learning were to be used to help effect change. He also told them that change came in a variety of guises:

> We have two choices with change in our lives. Whether we like it or not, we're not going to be able to hide from it. Either we're going to be change agents and effect change, or we're going to become its victims. I used to guarantee everyone that we would either all be doing something different within six

months, or we would all be doing the same thing differently. That's why the tools from the PITT Workshop were imperative if we were to take the business to the next level.

I would talk to them about our management team, and I would ask them to give me a vote on where we were as managers, because we needed to change too. We needed to move from managing and controlling to leading and supporting. I'd ask them where they were in the four phases that we go through in a transformation:

- unconsciously incompetent
- consciously incompetent
- consciously competent
- unconsciously competent.

Everyone would laugh, and then we'd discuss which level of mastery the management team had achieved.

Bannon is an avid advocate of the effective use of measurements, which will be discussed in Chapter 10, 'Managing Information II':

If you have no way of measuring progress, then you are wandering in the dark and not effectively serving your customers.

Measurements are very important to much of what we do, day in and day out, whether at work or play. Who plays golf and doesn't look at the score until the very end? You keep measuring so that you can make adjustments to reach your final goal. Take a baseball game, for example. The players keep looking at the score, and adjust their strategy based upon the score. They check the score throughout the game.

I really believe that if it's worth doing, it's worth measuring.

But Bannon notes that measurements need to be used wisely:

If the measurements that your manager is asking for are not helping you to assess and adjust your performance, then you need to ask just what the heck is the reason for taking the measurement?

Sometimes the measurements are worse than useless, because they can be detrimental to the goal.

> One team was preparing a monthly performance review that ran to 70 pages. It took them one full day on the second pass of the review.

This was definitely a case of information overload, which we will discuss in Chapter 9, 'Managing Information I'.

> If a measurement can't be used to improve performance, then it needs to be challenged to see whether it is really necessary. The team with the 70-page review did exactly that. When they revised their measurements and included only those that served a real purpose in improving performance, they were able to eliminate 50 of the 70 pages, and saved four people a day's work every month. On further review, I even questioned why 20 pages were necessary.

Bannon followed his own precepts by creating a score card to measure the work of the team workshops:

> We built that score card as we went along, so I could go back to my managers and say, 'Here's how many hours I've saved as the result of this workshop.'

Mind Mapping is just one of the skills that Bannon and his staff acquired to deal with all the changes needed to bring about the new alignment. In doing that, Bannon was making a conscious investment in the company's human assets, something to be discussed in Chapter 2, 'Intellectual Capital'. He created an environment that facilitated learning, encouraged creativity, opened communication channels, and lived it all through teamwork.

The name of the game

In working to implement all these new ideas, Bannon made effective use of the Brain Principle of persistence (see Chapter 3, 'Our Creative Brain'):

> I have a saying: **'Repetition is the name of the game.'** You can't introduce a new idea once and assume that everyone is going to begin immediately putting it into practice. People get caught up in their day-to-day pressures and crises and just don't find the time to implement it. In some instances, they use the idea once but don't store it in their memory banks.

Bannon attended all 18 team workshops held during a two-year period. He spent the entire last day of each workshop listening to the presentations that the participants made, which consisted of a discussion of their activities, the selection of an activity for analysis, the Mind Map of the problems, the proposed solutions, and the action plan. During the workshops, Bannon would tell the presenters that because so many opportunities for improvement had been identified, if he tried single-handedly to solve all the problems, nothing would happen:

> There is too much going on, and what I really need to do is to find out how I can help you do what needs to be done. You're my customers. Tell me what I can do to help you implement your action plans.

The following example is from a team of payroll specialists led by Mary Rose Cerrone who attended one of the PITT Workshops sponsored by Bannon. This team selected a reconciliation activity for improvement. (See Figure 1.1 on page 9.)

The 980/981 reconciliation activity ensures that for each payroll transaction, the amount recorded in the accounting ledger equals the amount paid out to the employee. When the payroll team came into the workshop, they were frustrated about a problem they had been unable to resolve. Prior to the workshop, team members had been unable to articulate the full magnitude of the problem or recommend solutions.

When Bannon saw their workshop presentation of the Mind Map, his immediate response was:

> I finally understand what the team has been trying to communicate, and I know what action should be taken to help them.

He used their team Mind Map to communicate the issues to the systems support team, suggesting the action steps required to address them. The result was a major reduction in workload, which encouraged the team members to continue applying these new tools on other projects.

Bannon also made personal use of the news skills and tools, Mind Maps in particular:

> When I started going to the final day of the workshops, I usually had five or six pages of notes about what I wanted to say. I would fumble through them, and I didn't do a very good job

of presenting. As I learned about Mind Mapping, I ended up building myself a Mind Map. Its central image constantly reminded me to do less talking and more listening. I would come in and use that to demonstrate to my managers and staff that I was using the same tools that they learned in the class.

Bannon's Mind Map's central image was a big 'C', representing the Customers that Bannon was serving: his employees.

I always thanked everyone, and I made sure they understood that they were a key customer of mine. I told my boss not to book an appointment on my calendar when one of these workshops was occurring, because this was the one meeting on my calendar that could never be changed!

It was important that the workshop participants knew that I was there to listen more than talk. I told them that my mother used to tell me when I was going to school that 'No news is good news.' She never wanted to hear from my teacher.

But as I grew older and wiser, I altered this philosophy when it comes to business. No news is *not* good news. If you aren't talking to me, it usually means there's a problem. It is my job to create an environment that is open enough for you to tell me about what's going on, even when it is unfavourable. So if I leave a workshop with no new information, then I'm going to leave disappointed, feeling that I've failed.

By and large, I never left with no new news.

This is the principle of feedback which will be discussed in Chapter 6, 'TEFCAS: The Success Formula'.

Bannon admits that creativity used to be a challenge, both for him and others in the organization:

People would say, 'Well, I'm not creative.' Hell, I used to say it myself. But I recognized that such a statement was an inhibitor. I talked myself through this, and realized that being creative didn't necessarily mean that you had to generate a new idea yourself. It is just as creative to take someone else's idea and apply it to a new situation. From personal experience I found that I could take someone else's idea and improve it before I applied it to a new situation. I have a knack for what

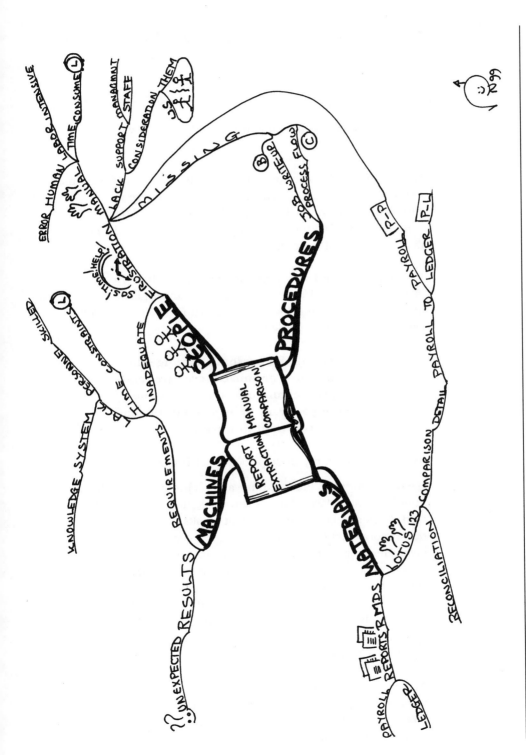

Figure 1.1 The 980/981 Reconciliation Mind Map

I call 'connecting the dots': taking different situations, different experiences, different ideas, combining them in a unique way, and – boom – forming a new idea.

That happens all the time in teams:

I used to see that same thing in the workshops. It was electrifying.

Because of the diversity of teams, ideas just spring off the table. You take something from here, from there – different situations, different backgrounds, different ideas. The combinations of all those inputs generate new ideas. To me, that's the greatest form of creativity.

I remember when I was a first line manager, I had five characteristics that I used to look for in people that would make them successful. I wrote this down in 1976, and I still carry the list around with me:

> **A successful person is intelligent,**
> **industrious, organized, creative, and**
> **a good communicator. That's the**
> **person you want to be around, the one**
> **you want to work with.**

Bannon continues to apply these principles at Entex:

We didn't start the Process Innovation Through Teams here until November 1997. Since then, we've done a couple of workshops and have achieved great results. The workshops boost morale, and raise the sense people have of purpose and involvement in identifying and addressing issues. It's unbelievable! They really understand that senior management cares what they think; they get to choose the projects they want to work on. Occasionally I don't think the project they select is critical, but even in that instance they are improving their skills. I expect them to succeed and use their experience on a bigger project next time.

At Entex, I have been working with the senior management team to recognize the difference between an activity and a process (see Chapter 11). We emphasize that we have to start looking at things at the process level. That means you need to break down organizational boundaries. I don't really care whether the problem is a purchasing problem or an accounts payable problem, it's still part of the procurement process.

We make sure that we have members from different organizations on our teams. For example, if we have trouble with returns to one of our manufacturers, we use somebody from inventory management, someone from the field – a salesperson or someone in a branch office – and someone from finance. I'd never just have finance people working on a problem.

Teams help you connect the dots. At IBM, we would have several teams, one from payroll, one from travel expense accounting, one from accounts payable, one from inter-company accounting, and one from our international accounting group. There was always a diverse group, working on different problems.

What really helped everyone was listening to each others' problems, challenges and opportunities as they were presented to the group. In one case, a team had a payroll problem, and the deliverable was a payroll cheque. Another team had an accounts payable issue, and they'd talk about how they had exceptions to their process, where they had to do a manual work-around. It's a matter of synergy.

The principles outlined in this book are not something to be used once and then put away. Bannon knows the value of follow-through. He would go back to the workshop teams, review what they had done, and then bring the teams in to present to his boss:

I made my reviews as informal as I could so it wouldn't appear as if I were checking up on them. That was never a problem. They *wanted* the opportunity to show me what they were doing. They created their own measurements of their progress. They created deliverables that were tangible and measurable, and measurements that they were eager to show me.

The culture change here was very important. We created the opportunity for the teams to present the action plans to my boss because I didn't want to take the credit for their work. I wanted the people who were actually doing the work to receive the recognition.

The first meeting that we had with my boss was very difficult because he was not in the mood to look at Mind Maps. But one team member, Rosanne Grano, stood up in front of him, and demonstrated a sense of leadership that I had never expected from her and had never seen from someone at her level in the organization. She stood tall and remained confident whenever he challenged her, and all of a sudden the people in the audience started supporting her. The swell was incredible. There was a leader born right there in front of my eyes. Once I supported her and told her what she had done, she just continued to grow. She is a remarkable young lady. That was just one example of many.

Bannon faced many problems, but he always kept going:

What motivated me to continue was seeing the power that comes from developing an overall vision, a road map. I was able to set up a score card that allowed me to measure whether or not I was making progress, and if the progress was accelerating or decelerating. That allowed me to make adjustments along the way.

Another thing is that I don't mind failing. You're going to fail now and then. But you just have to get up, dust yourself off, and try again. It's not only the ideas you have as a leader that are important. It's persistence and determination that leads to success. (See Chapters 3 and 6.)

Whenever anyone told me that I was a failure or that I was not succeeding, I would ask myself: 'What did I learn from the experience?' You have to reinforce the positive rather than the negative. I was told at certain times of my life that I couldn't do something. I couldn't go to a certain school because I wasn't smart enough. I couldn't play this sport because I wasn't big enough. I couldn't dance because I didn't have rhythm. Those doomsayers never helped me accomplish anything.

Now I surround myself with people who say, 'Hey, if you really want to do it, you can do it. Believe in yourself.'

Sarah Wilson, Manager of General Accounting at Entex, and her team were imbued with that same spirit after Bannon introduced his vision during a workshop at Entex.

Wilson's workshop chose as its first project the automating of a highly manual task, the distribution of departmental profit and loss reports to departmental managers twice a month. The reports were first drawn up using the company's mainframe computer, an employee would then have to spend a day printing, reconciling, copying and collating them, and they were then hand-delivered, or sent via overnight courier to remote locations.

The workshop group decided to prepare the reports so that they could be sent electronically directly to people's workstations. To make the presentation of the electronic reports more useful and appealing, the group decided to prepare them in *Excel* spreadsheet format.

Since many recipients had been keying the data from the original hard-copy reports into their spreadsheets for analysis anyway, receiving an electronic version of the report would save them time and effort. Moreover, it might encourage those who hadn't been doing any analysis to do so.

'All told, including meeting with Rich Bannon, we probably invested about four person-days in this project,' Wilson notes:

> Since the staff person was spending two days per month on this manual collating task, the payback was realized in just two months. Those two days a month are now available for this person to do more valuable tasks. In addition to the time savings, there were also modest cost savings due to less paper being used and elimination of overnight deliveries of these statements.

The recipients of the new reports were very pleased, and immediately saw the possibilities, says Wilson:

> We have now been asked to incorporate more information into the reports (comparing current period to prior-year data), and we have also been asked to provide a comparison to latest forecasts. This is exactly what we had hoped would happen: it has encouraged people to take a fresh look at the data and is spurring more analysis and understanding of the results that we are reporting. We will be incorporating these suggestions in our future reporting.

> We also intend to use the process [see Chapter 11] we developed to distribute other reports so we can leverage the work we have already done to provide us with additional improvements with little effort.

Wilson reports that the new ideas that Bannon introduced had a very positive influence on Entex employees:

> Everyone felt very good about it. They were pleased at our ability to achieve our goals, and they were pleased at the positive feedback we've got from the new process. So I think people are motivated to move on to the next project. They are eager to work on the next thing.

Bannon's experiences with the Brain Principles, Mind Mapping and TEFCAS have left him with strong convictions about the future of business.

Looking to the future

Rich Bannon has some tips for the business leaders of the future:

> I think the business leaders of the future need to move away from the 'command and control' style of managing, where they have to be the centre of expertise on every single item. It will be impossible for them to know the exact progress of their people on every detailed activity at every single moment. Instead, they need to create an environment that promotes creativity, growth, learning, responsibility and teamwork.
>
> The business world has changed so dramatically that you can't be an expert or be up to date on everything. You have to create an environment in which people feel comfortable bringing you problems or admitting they made a mistake. The accountability comes in learning from them, and not repeating the same errors. That's one of the things we learned from the TEFCAS model, and the other Brain Principles described in this book.

Rich Bannon is certainly a BrainSmart Leader, and the formula he used to achieve this status is revealed in the chapters that follow.

So, what happened to Bannon's teams once he left IBM and moved to Entex? We shall return to that later.

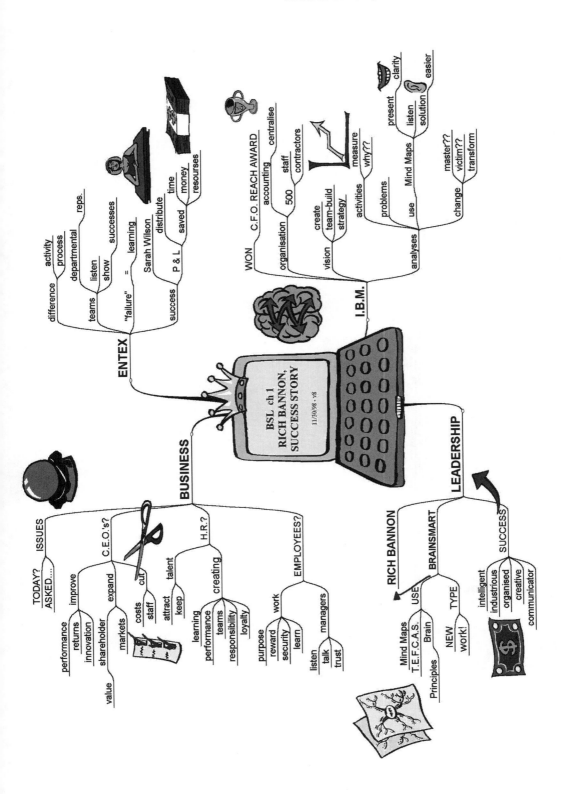

2 INTELLECTUAL CAPITAL

Quiz

1. Human intelligence is the primary driver of change. True or False?

2. The rate of change in your company/industry will increase in the next five years. True or False?

3. If you don't invest in human intelligence you can still stay ahead of your competition. True or False?

4. Managing your career and skill set is your responsibility. True or False?

5. You can solve some of your toughest problems while you are sleeping. True or False?

6. During the last 25 years the number of people working in brain research has grown from 500 to more than 30 000. True or False?

7. Ninety per cent of everything we know about the human brain has been learned in the last 10 years. True or False?

8. The ability to use colour enhances your memory. True or False?

9. You are born creative and it's not a faculty you can develop. True or False?

10. Educational systems stress the importance of whole brain thinking. True or False?

SCORING

Give yourself two points for every question you answered correctly. The correct answer in every case, except Questions 3, 9 and 10, is 'True'. If you have scored 18 or more, this chapter will help you refine your BrainSmart Leadership skills. If you scored less than 18, this chapter will help you begin to define your BrainSmart Leadership development.

Overview

Businesses are at the forefront of the revolution in thinking. In an environment that is global, complex and competitive, we look at some of the advantages accruing to a company which recognizes that human resources are the key to long-term success.

Assets in the billions

Imagine your company owns a computer with the ability to receive and transmit information using a variety of input/output devices, such as visual, auditory and tactile. It has unlimited memory available, with built-in redundancies to ensure that vital data is never lost. How much would that computer be worth if it could use this combination of input devices and storage capacity to continually add to its database of knowledge? How much would that computer be worth if it could use the knowledge it gained from experience to re-program itself, so that mistakes were less likely to be repeated? And how much would that computer be worth if it had the ability to program other computers so that they also learned from its experiences? How much would that computer be worth to your company? Millions? Billions?

As you are reading these sentences, you are using the most powerful tool ever known. Your brain is that computer – worth billions! Our research and experience have consistently demonstrated that the brain's capabilities are greatly under-exploited. We have also seen the dramatic improvements possible when the brain's capabilities are used more fully.

If your company had assets worth billions and you learned that only one per cent of that asset's capacity was being used, would that worry you? If the efficiency of that asset improved tenfold, how much would that add to the profitability of your company?

Intelligence: the lever that can move the world

Is it possible that Jack Welch, who has led General Electric for more than fifteen years, has been using such a computer? Despite being in a mature industry, GE has performed significantly better than its competitors because it has focused on productivity, improving its merchandise, and generating savings. The secret of Welch's success is revealed by a comment he made in 1994:

> There is infinite potential for savings. The human mind is always able to find a better way to do things.

GE and other successful companies know that technology alone is not enough. They realize that it is the ability of people to harness their natural intelligence to create and apply technology that is responsible for generating extraordinary financial results. They understand that technology is the result of the application of human intelligence.

> We believe that successful businesses have always depended on brains, and that thinking, creativity and communication will continue to drive the innovative corporation towards success, to survive, to prosper, to innovate and to succeed – to soar beyond all competition.

Astute companies know that future success depends on an intangible resource – the *Intellectual Capital* within the organization. Successful corporations in the future will be intelligence-driven, realizing that intelligence is not just capacity – stored knowledge – but also the ability to make the most of it. The sum of these two is the organization's Intellectual Capital, and harnessing it will create the competitive advantage.

CASE STUDY

Gonzalo Somarriba

The roomful of people waited expectantly. Ten of them had just passed an aptitude test for job openings at Rinker, a construction materials company manufacturing everything from concrete blocks to cement which has 21 000 employees in its four main markets: China, Australia, the USA and Pakistan.

These candidates were applying for entry-level unskilled and semi-skilled jobs at minimum wages! They had little education, and many had never seen a computer, but now they faced the harsh reality of the new business world. 'We are a thinking organization. We want you to think, to be able to ask questions, not to be afraid of the technology you will be trained to use, especially the computers that now drive our business,' said a reassuring Gonzalo Somarriba, Rinker's Miami Manager of Human Resources, as he handed out application forms.

Turning towards Richard Israel, he said: 'Richard, we face a constant onslaught of new technology. We are spending over $800 million on technological upgrades to our plant and equipment in Miami alone in the next twelve months. We must hire people who can think for themselves and learn to use computers.'

The silence in that small, crowded conference room at the Department of Labor in Hialeah, Miami, indicated the impact of his words. These were low-paid jobs in Dade County, where there were eighty applications for every advertised vacancy. And Rinker's jobs required you to be fluent in English and Spanish, as well as computer-literate!

'We are an excellent company to work for. We expect you to work hard and be loyal, and in return you can expect the same.' Brushing over the low entry-level pay, Gonzalo concentrated on the benefits: 'We have an excellent medical programme. We promote from within, and we encourage you to study with extensive educational reimbursement programmes.'

Richard was struck by Gonzalo's emphasis on the need to become computer-literate. Rinker's equipment and trucks were all computer-controlled, so even truck drivers needed to improve their skills and increase their intellectual capital.

It is time for you to make an inventory of your firm's Intellectual Capital; and then learn how to make it grow. When you release the intelligence of your workforce, some of the advantages you will enjoy include:

- enthusiastic employees
- increased creativity
- the ability to create change, rather than react to it
- taking advantage of the information explosion
- the effective use of technology
- making people accountable for results.

Our marvellous brain

Our brain is the most complex and wondrous device ever designed, capable of storing more bits of information than the most powerful supercomputer. However, the brain doesn't work like a computer. We don't turn it on when we arrive at work and off when we leave. We see evidence of this in our lives every day. How many times have you had an idea about an important work issue while you were not at work, perhaps in the shower or when you suddenly awoke at 3 a.m.? This happens because the brain works 24 hours a day to achieve the goals we tell it are important. Imagine how much more you could achieve, if you could learn to improve how it works. What if simply learning more about how your brain works could help you grow in both your personal and professional life?

Over 95 per cent of everything we know about the human brain has been learned in the last ten years. Advances in medical research have made it possible for the first time to study the inner workings of the brain. In 1980, scientists believed that we used 5 per cent of our brain's ability. By the end of the decade, many scientists argued that the proportion was 1 per cent. Today, many believe that we use even less than that, and all agree that the potential for improving on this is enormous.

During the past twenty-five years, the number of people working in the field of brain research has grown from 500 to over 30 000, according to Ronald Kotulak, author of *Inside the Brain*. The brain has been featured on magazine covers more often during the 1990s than at any other time, and cover stories in publications such as *Time, Newsweek, New Scientist, Discover, Omni* and *National Geographic* have chronicled many of the breakthroughs and puzzles uncovered.

What if, as a result of all this research, new tools could be created to revolutionize the way we view work? What if we were all born naturally creative? What if the more we learned, the easier it was to learn more? What if the people who have been telling us that we can't learn to do certain things are wrong?

Well, this book argues that all these statements are true. The fruits of this research are a technology that enables us to increase our intellectual capital. As with any new technology, at first it may be difficult for society to adapt to it and the changes it brings. A few pioneers will try it out, and as their discoveries prove worthwhile and more people learn of them, it will cause a snowball effect, until eventually, the majority of the population will adopt the technology.

During this pioneering stage of the study of human intelligence, there may be many struggles, hardships and setbacks to deal with. Yet those who persist will reap great rewards.

What is PITT, and how was it created?

While training to become a licensed instructor of Tony Buzan's Mental Literacy Principles, Tony Dottino realized that they offered companies the opportunity to tap the enormous potential of the human brain to create the ultimate competitive advantage. He created a comprehensive programme using Tony Buzan's Brain Principles (Mental Literacy), process management, and the synergistic energy of teams, all of which are described in this book. As part of this programme, Dottino created a new workshop, Process Innovation Through Teams (PITT), which he has used with groups in top-level companies to tap the enormous potential of the human brain, unleash their creative energies and establish the ultimate competitive advantage. These groups go on to achieve remarkable, measurable results. More importantly, as the word of their achievements spreads throughout the company and more groups undergo this transformation, entire business divisions deliver increasingly positive results.

The experience from these workshops has consistently revealed that companies usually spend about 25–30 per cent of their resources working on problems, correcting errors many times, and in the worst case, throwing everything away and starting anew. But what if the creative teamwork of an enterprise could be geared to developing ways to eliminate this wasted capacity and apply it to new market opportunities? What might that do to the need for downsizing? Chapter 11 covers PITT in detail.

Rich Bannon, Senior Vice President and Corporate Controller of Entex (see Chapter 1), summarized his own experiences with these techniques:

> The tools offered by the PITT approach are what we need if we are to take our business to the next level of competition. Applying the Brain Principles [see Chapter 3], Mind Mapping [see Chapter 4] and Process Innovation [see Chapter 11] to tap into the unlimited potential of human thinking provides a true competitive advantage.

The global economy creates pressure to reduce costs

The relentless competition unleashed by the growing international fight for market share means that companies are under constant pressure to lower prices while improving product quality and service. Because of this, the consumer has greater choice than ever when selecting a product from global channels of distribution. The need to remain competitive in the marketplace has resulted in a wave of downsizing, restructuring and cost-cutting, but we believe that maximizing Intellectual Capital offers an alternative to downsizing. Remaining competitive in the future will rely on investment in developing brain power.

THE IMPACT OF DOWNSIZING ON CREATIVITY

Corporate downsizing frequently results in a small reduction in work and a large reduction in workforce. The remaining employees are left with more work than ever, and become too busy with their jobs to think about how to improve what they are doing.

A common lament is: 'I haven't got time for creative thinking, I have too much to do.' Creativity is left to somebody else – who, unfortunately, is probably just as busy. Do you feel this way? Have you heard – or possibly spoken – these words?

Another problem caused by downsizing is that the survivors tend to be less willing to take risks. Having escaped the axe for the time being, they avoid making waves or taking risks. They are fearful of generating new ideas because they could be ridiculed and viewed as impractical – or even worse, the ideas might fail. They believe that someone who is not seen to be busy could be targeted for additional work or the next round of redundancies. In reality, to be creative you need time to contemplate, which allows your brain to incubate and generate creative answers.

The irony is that at a time when creative thinking and innovation are more important than ever, in many instances they are in shorter supply than ever.

Technology and Downsizings call for Greater Individual Responsibility.

The current economic reality has shattered any idea of a 'job for life'. Individuals are now responsible for managing their own careers and updating their skills. How many people have come to terms with this new reality? How many are equipped to deal with it? This raises a central issue: where have we been taught to make the most of our brain's potential? Certainly not in most of the Western school system. The number one problem facing society today is the poor quality of the education system, and the resulting lack of skills among the workforce.

The income gap between knowledge and non-knowledge workers has widened in the last ten years, and is likely to continue to do so. People who do not invest in their own Intellectual Capital face a gloomy future. The scarcity of knowledge workers will result in labour shortages and severely limit opportunities for companies that want to expand in both their domestic and global marketplaces.

The advantages of applying Brain Principles

Current business practices fail to draw on knowledge of how the brain processes information. In many if not most instances, people work without making the best use of their natural intelligence. In fact, organizational structures and policies frequently work against basic Brain Principles. For example:

- Management teams don't establish a clear goal or vision.
- Executives don't want to receive 'bad news', or are insulated from it.
- Work teams are formed which lack a balance of technical and interpersonal skills and experience.
- Information is withheld from the people who need it most.

Any company that learns to meet these challenges by applying Brain Principles will secure a significant advantage.

Leadership profile: Bruce Wagner

Take Bruce Wagner, for example, currently the manager of IBM North America's Accounting Consolidation and Measurements Department. Bruce was first exposed to the principles set out in this book when he was the manager of IBM's World Trade Accounting Services Organization. His responsibilities at the time included the inter-company billings process covering $26 billion dollars' worth of goods and services world-wide.

He saw the need for his organization to maintain their skills in process analysis, particularly during this period, when IBM was reducing resources and consolidating organizations.

In 1995, Bruce attended a Process Innovation Through Teams (PITT) Workshop (see Chapter 11). He also learned about Brain Principles (see Chapter 3) and their application to business and accounting processes. He found the skills he learned in these sessions so valuable that he sent his entire staff to the training sessions. Next, he created over fifteen teams to work on various elements of the inter-company process. These teams were able to identify and implement process innovations which resulted in savings of over 585 person-hours per month for his organization.

After moving into his current position, Bruce continued to apply the same Brain Principles, Mind Mapping and Process Innovation techniques that had proved so successful, and uses them to achieve the same remarkable business results. As he confidently states:

> Give a problem to the brain to solve, and it will look for the best solution. Give that problem to a team, and the

combination of the various experiences and the mix of cortical skills [see Chapter 4] will increase the creative power of the team and help them towards the best solution.

Conclusion

Any company which applies Brain Principles to business issues will secure a competitive advantage. Their workforce will be focused on a common mission, excited about where they are going, and constantly learning from one another. On that basis, they will continue to generate the intellectual capital that will sustain profitable growth.

ACTIVITIES

1. **How much effort (as a percentage of 100) do you think people at your company apply to their work? Why do you think this is the case?**

2. **Do you believe there is a lack of loyalty towards your organization by employees today? If your answer is yes, then how do you think it can be earned back?**

3. **List all the different initiatives your company has used over the last few years to improve productivity and what results were achieved.**

4. **Look at the annual report of 10 major companies and highlight all the references that are made to Intellectual Capital. How does your company measure against this?**

5. Visit your nearest bookshop and look at the number of books and magazines written about the brain and current research findings. Select one that interests you, buy it, and read it. After finishing the book or magazine, list the applications that this research has in your work environment.

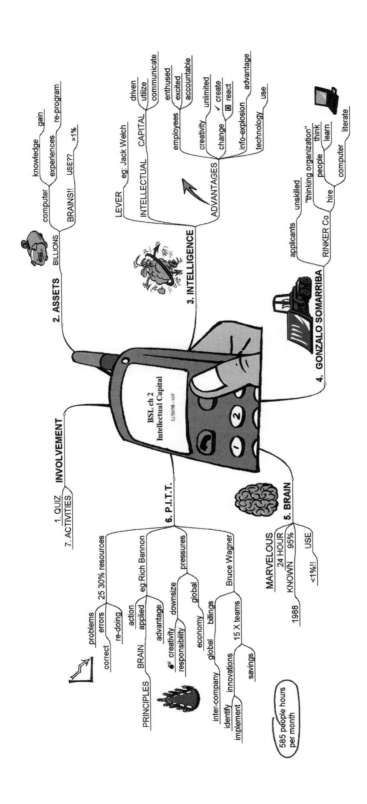

BSL ch 2
Intellectual Capital
11/30/98 - v10

2. ASSETS

computer — knowledge — gain
      — experiences — re-program
BILLIONS — BRAINS!! — USE?? — >1%

3. INTELLIGENCE

LEVER — eg: Jack Welch

INTELLECTUAL CAPITAL
    — employees — driven
      — utilize
      — communicate
      — enthused
      — excited
      — accountable

ADVANTAGES
    — creativity — unlimited
    — change — ✓ create
      — ☒ react
    — info-explosion — advantage
    — technology — use

4. GONZALO SOMARRIBA

applicants — unskilled
  — "thinking organization"
RINKER Co — people — think
  — hire — learn
  — computer — literate

1. QUIZ   INVOLVEMENT

7. ACTIVITIES

6. P.I.T.T.

PRINCIPLES
  — problems
correct — errors — re-doing
  — 25 30% resources
BRAIN — action — applied — eg: Rich Bannon
  — advantage
  — creativity
  — responsibility
  — downsize — pressures — global
  — economy — global
  — global — billings
identify — innovations — 15 X teams — Bruce Wagner
implement — inter-company — savings

585 people hours
per month

5. BRAIN

MARVELOUS
KNOWN — 24 HOUR — 95%
1988 — USE — <1%!!

3 OUR CREATIVE BRAIN

1. Your brain operates on the principle 'Garbage in, Garbage out'.

   True or False?

2. It is possible to take one new thought and create a thousand new ideas from it.

   True or False?

3. You can achieve anything your brain can imagine provided it has the right information.

   True or False?

4. Written goals help your brain to focus on actions necessary to achieving them.

   True or False?

5. A fast way to learn is to mimic successful people.

   True or False?

6. If you don't have all the information on a given subject, your brain creates answers (right or wrong) to 'complete the picture'.

   True or False?

7. Your brain needs new ideas as a form of nourishment, just as your body needs food.

   True or False?

8. Your brain searches for the truth in the information it receives.

   True or False?

9. Your brain is preprogrammed to be persistent in reaching outcomes, provided that you know what you want.

   True or False?

10. If you supply your brain with new information it will perform better.

    True or False?

SCORING

The correct answer in every case except Question 1 is 'True'. Give yourself two points for every question you answered correctly.

If you scored 18 points or more, you have an excellent understanding of the subject and this chapter will help you refine your skills. If you scored less than 18, this chapter will add significantly to your leadership development.

Overview

In this chapter, we describe the seven Brain Principles in practical terms. We show the benefits a company enjoys when it applies each principle correctly, and the penalty it suffers when it does not. We conclude the chapter with a description of the exciting result that occurs when the seven principles are working in harmony – the generation of natural creativity and innovation.

Brain Principles

Despite your brain's amazing complexity, only seven principles govern its responses. Each of these principles is a part of the operating system your bio-computer – for that is what the brain is – uses for all its thinking and learning.

The Seven Brain Principles

1. The brain synergizes information, so that 1 plus 1 is two or more.
2. The brain is a success-driven mechanism.
3. The brain has the ability to mimic actions perfectly.
4. The brain craves completeness (it needs to fill in the blanks).
5. The brain constantly seeks new knowledge and information.
6. The brain is truth-seeking.
7. The brain is persistent.

Brain Principle 1: The brain synergizes information, so that 1 plus 1 is two or more

Research has shown that the brain has synergistic powers. This means that one thought triggers another, which in turn triggers another, and so on. Imagine receiving a message at work saying that an urgent letter has arrived at home. How many different thoughts will be triggered in your mind by this initial piece of information? This is divergent thinking: our ability to start from one central idea and to move onto many ideas. It means we are capable of creating our own internal universes of knowledge, networks of thought, memory banks, and uniquely innovative and inspirational ideas. Convergent thinking on the other hand (which is what is measured by most IQ tests), is our ability to narrow from many ideas to one, such as selecting one vendor from a list of twenty.

When the brain is vigorously thinking and learning, each neuron develops more connections (axons and dendrites – see Chapter 8) to communicate with other neurons. This process creates a more sophisticated, intricate and complex bio-computer. What we think, the way we think and the way we think about thinking literally change the biological structure of our brain.

Creativity occurs when the brain's synergistic ability combines and links existing knowledge with new ideas to create new thought patterns. It happens naturally when members of an organization exchange ideas and direction. Synergy explains why new ideas and associations fed into the existing knowledge base lead to breakthroughs in creative thinking.

The brain's ability to synthesize new and existing information explains the acceleration of technological innovation. Because each generation of people start with all the accumulated knowledge of their predecessors, we have a knowledge base upon which to build. Each new breakthrough or discovery of information adds to that knowledge base, so that the pace of technological advancement and creative thinking accelerates. An example of this is the advances made in computer hardware and software over the last fifteen years. Communication vehicles such as the Internet which can transfer knowledge and experience between users from around the globe mean that the rate of change will accelerate exponentially.

Lack of familiarity with this principle sometimes causes frustration for those who attend a business or self-improvement seminar or read a book on this topic, who frequently complain: 'Most of the material I already knew! I didn't learn much new!' – and they stop thinking. If they applied their knowledge of synergy it would mean that even if 99 per cent of the material was familiar, the 1 per cent which is new will trigger new associations and ideas. These associations will build upon existing knowledge to create new ideas, which will in turn create more new ideas. Even one new idea or thought from a seminar or book can eventually generate a breakthrough idea. That is why we stress that every person can trigger valuable ideas – listen to all of them.

SYNERGY FOLLOWS THE *GIGG* PROCESS

You may be familiar with the computer acronym GIGO – Garbage In, Garbage Out – and apply it to your thinking. However, we feel another acronym reflects the synergy principle more accurately: GIGG (negative). Based upon what you now know about the brain's structure, what do you think happens when the brain has garbage entered into it? Because of the synergy of the brain:

Garbage In, Garbage Grows.

Our brain builds a garbage dump which accumulates all the junk it receives. All new junk entered is added to the dump, and the dump grows exponentially because of synergy. Negative thinking, pessimism and cynicism breed more of the same. Imagine the implications of this if you and your employees expend most of your mental energy on negative and cynical thoughts about your company. That thinking will become more prevalent until it pervades the organization, turning your own creative energy against your company and yourself!

The opposite of 'Garbage In, Garbage Grows' is GIGG (positive):

Good In, Good Grows towards a
positive outcome.

Just as the brain's synergy can be destructive when fed negative thoughts, it becomes radiant when given positive inputs. A person whose brain is synergizing positive thoughts to generate more positive, creative thoughts is using what we call 'Radiant Thinking'. We use this term because a brain working in this fashion becomes like a sun, radiating light in all directions.

This means that as well as being self-destructive, the brain can be self-enhancing. It is important to recognize that in most instances, we control the information entered into our brain. We control what the Gs in GIGG will represent.

Brain Principle 2: The brain is a success-driven mechanism

When you set a goal, your brain will guide your thought processes, consciously and unconsciously, in a direction that helps you achieve

BrainSmart!

Use these methods to maximize the benefits of synergy:

- Focus clearly on your goals.
- Learn to recognize and select appropriate positive inputs for your brain.
- Learn a new skill.
- See the positive in situations.

success. The more precisely and consistently you define your goal, the easier it is for your brain to develop an effective strategy. That is why it is vital to describe your desired outcome sufficiently clearly that it can be visualized and referred to later as you measure your progress.

How many times have you heard someone stress the importance of writing down goals as a tool for success? Yet fewer than 10 per cent of those we have encountered have done so. Why is writing down goals important?

The act of writing down a goal and then reading it clarifies and reinforces the message. Without this additional emphasis, the criteria of success can become distorted.

This Brain Principle also explains the importance of having clearly defined customer requirements. During our encounters with Total Quality Management (TQM), we have found that companies with a clear definition of customer requirements consistently outperform those whose customer requirements are ambiguous or confusing.

Do you work for a company which has clearly defined customer requirements that you can state, or are you in the frustrating position of not knowing them? How many times have you been asked, 'What are you trying to do?' How many times have you wondered, 'What is the goal I am trying to reach?'

In order for your brain to work at its optimal level, you must provide it with clearly defined end results and criteria to evaluate its progress. When allocating time priorities on a work project, make sure you allow time to write your goals down: because it will have a tremendous impact on your effectiveness. If possible, create images of what the finished product will look like. Encourage yourself to write down additional goals too, since they provide fuel for creative thinking.

BrainSmart!

Use these methods to maximize the effectiveness of your success-driven mechanism:

- Develop a clear, documented vision of your goals. This provides you with several benefits:
  - It forces you to clarify your thinking by eliminating any ambiguity about what you want to achieve.
  - It stimulates creativity by making your brain think imaginatively about goal definition and goal fulfilment.
  - It reinforces your commitment to achieving the goal by strengthening its imprint in your brain.
- Check and note your progress regularly.
- Establish interim milestones, and celebrate small successes along the way.

Brain Principle 3: The brain has the ability to mimic actions perfectly

Copying the work of others is usually considered cheating during formal education, but this does not apply in the workplace. The brain learns best by copying others. The brain has the ability to learn new skills quickly by imitating others who are proficient at that skill and studying and imitating someone else's work helps you improve your existing skills. Unless you are taking a test to measure your knowledge, copying is OK! Trying to learn without taking advantage of this Brain Principle is counter-productive. Imagine an infant trying to learn to speak, and being told by its parent, 'Don't copy the words Mummy just said to you! That's cheating! Make up your own!'

To see this Brain Principle in action, observe an infant learning a new skill. The infant studies the role model intently, trying to duplicate the behaviour exactly as modelled. Using this ability, plus Brain Principle 7 – persistence (see page 40) – the infant learns the new skill quickly through closely observing and mimicking practice.

Our brain works both consciously and unconsciously to duplicate behaviour and skill performance to perfection by searching for a model to imitate.

After identifying an acceptable model, it consciously studies the behaviour and mimics it.

The brain also copies behaviours on an unconscious level. When we listen to someone speak, the brain unconsciously detects the speaker's favourite phrases and mannerisms. Without even realizing it, we start mimicking them, often using the same phrases.

During a recent meeting with an executive team, several managers made a presentation of an operating plan to the chief executive officer. The CEO of this company frequently uses the word 'remarkable' to describe data or behaviour which is either unusual or impressive. In the presentation of the operating plan, each presenter used the word 'remarkable' – an average of six times during each ten-minute presentation. Remarkable!

We need to be more aware of our brain's natural ability to mimic activities, otherwise we may begin mimicking inappropriate or poorly performed behaviours. We may not even realize that we are mimicking the behaviour until we have 'perfected' it. If this occurs, we will have to consciously search for a new, more appropriate model to follow, to replace the old. The longer this old, unacceptable behaviour has been established, the longer it will usually take for the new, acceptable behaviour to replace it, (see Chapter 6, TEFCAS).

The mimic principle means that the thinking patterns of our brains will reflect the environment in which we exist. Many experts on psychology and self-improvement advise that to become more successful, we should associate with successful people. To apply this knowledge, we should examine our associates and note the behaviours we are duplicating. Do they provide us with a model for success, or are they modelling inappropriate behaviours?

By combining the mimic and synergy principles, you can create a formula your brain will follow to achieve success, but you must do this consciously. For example, do you deliberately select your role models and associates, or do you just 'go with the flow'? Are you careful when selecting reading material or television programmes to view? Do you search for people who are already successful at a goal you desire, and examine their behaviour?

Now that you understand the mimic principle, consider the impact of lunchtime conversations spent with co-workers bombarding you with negative thoughts about the workplace. The mimic principle means that

BrainSmart!

Use these methods to maximize the benefits of mimicking:

- Associate as often as possible with people you respect.
- When a conversation in a group of people becomes negative, attempt to keep it realistically positive.
- Remove yourself from conversations that are non-productive.
- Select suitable role models for the skills and attitudes you wish to develop.
- Repeat a successful strategy for your current goal.

your brain will begin to copy these attitudes until they are firmly entrenched. When you combine this with the synergy principle, the GIGG outcome is disastrous. If you associate with cynical, pessimistic people, you will programme your brain to think about all your experiences in a similar fashion. If you surround yourself with negative people, you will programme yourself for failure.

Now consider the opposite. If your brain is exposed to people who are successful, innovative and happy, it will mimic and learn those positive thought patterns. By associating with positive people, you program yourself for success.

Brain Principle 4: The brain craves completeness – it needs to fill in the blanks

How many times have you heard someone begin a story and then pause, saying, 'I really shouldn't be telling you this.' Don't you feel like screaming, 'Get on with it! I want to know how it ends!' This happens because our brain craves completeness. When the brain is given incomplete information, it tries to fill in the blanks anyway.

The Greek philosopher Socrates often stimulated discussion and debate among his students by asking them challenging questions, and then responding with another question. He consistently made them aware of the gaps in their knowledge, which his students eagerly worked to fill. Hence the practice of using a series of questions to uncover the truth is often referred to as 'the Socratic method'.

The best managers are those who know how to ask the right questions, providing their employees with incomplete stories.

If you receive a message from your boss which says, 'Please see me at the end of the day', what does your brain do? It will not stop working until it generates an answer to the question, 'What does the boss want to see me about?'

This anxiety about what is going on explains the hours employees spend swapping rumours and searching for information on the corporate grapevine. When employees hear rumours about an organizational change, their brains crave an understanding of what is likely to happen. Another instance of no news is *not* good news!

The implications of this principle in day-to-day life are limitless. Think of all the people you communicate with on a daily basis and the words you use, the actions you take and the pictures you create in their minds. Imagine all the opportunities for misunderstandings that may have resulted.

Brain Principle 5: The brain constantly seeks new knowledge and information

Much like the rest of our body, our brain needs exercise to keep healthy and fit. It becomes stronger and more rigorous through the reinforcement of existing knowledge and the addition of new information. Like a well-conditioned athlete, the more you exercise your brain, the easier it is to perform difficult mental tasks. Furthermore, the more knowledge and information your brain possesses, the easier it becomes to learn new information.

When your brain is fed new relevant information, it remains fit and at the peak of its mental powers. If your brain is left to stagnate, it becomes flabby and sluggish. You lose some of your mental edge. By adding new information dendrites grow to enrich the brain (see Chapter 8).

Contrary to a popularly held belief, researchers have not found that learning new things becomes impossible with age. In fact, continuous learning throughout your lifetime may be one of the best ways to ensure that your brain remains healthy. A brain which is active and growing, even during later years, is much less likely to be susceptible to brain diseases which sap its

BrainSmart!

Use these methods to maximize the benefits of the completeness principle:

- To communicate effectively with someone, they need to have the same picture or image of what you've said as you have in your mind. Confirm this by asking them to describe the picture they have in their mind. This will provide you with feedback about how well you are communicating.
- After someone has requested you do something, check your understanding by repeating the request back to them.
- When brainstorming in a group, use as little detail as possible when trying to generate new ideas. By leaving many blanks, you will stimulate each person's mind to create solutions.
- Encourage completeness by beginning a sentence and letting others finish it for you.
- Celebrate the completion of something, such as a project or activity.

vitality. So it really is true: use it or lose it! As Warren Bennis insists in his book *Becoming a Leader*: 'You can learn anything you want to learn.'

One example which emphasizes the importance of continuing education in a profession is the licensing requirements for public accountants in the United States. Most states require that after reaching certification, the accountant complete an average of 40 hours study each year on topics related to the profession. This requirement encourages chartered accountants to maintain their professional expertise, and keeps their minds physically fit.

To provide a benefit, the new information you learn does not have to concern something which is familiar to you. In fact, learning about something totally different from your existing knowledge base can be a powerful way of spurring creativity. For example, if you are a finance specialist, learning about the marketing side of your organization will improve your financial skills. It will broaden your perspective and provide more data for your brain to analyse when studying financially related marketing issues. We call this 'making new connections' – taking different pieces of information and creating new associations between them.

Regardless of your profession, you need to realize that once your primary, secondary and higher education is over, your true learning has just begun.

BrainSmart!

Use the following methods to keep your brain fit:

- Read trade publications relevant to your profession at least several times per week.
- Meet with people in departments outside your functional area of expertise, and exchange ideas and knowledge.
- Take a course at a college or university on a topic which is of interest to you.
- Learn something new every day.
- Remember: you can learn at any age. Make the decision to keep learning.

Brain Principle 6: The brain is truth-seeking

In their book *Brain Sell*, Tony Buzan and Richard Israel introduce the idea of the brain as a truth-seeking instrument. For the brain, truth means survival, which is why it strives to learn or discover.

We can see instances of the importance of this every day in the behaviour of children. Why do they constantly demand fairness in their games? Why do they frequently ask the question 'Why?' Because the truth is accurate information, and the brain is hungry for that information.

Imagine that a man is crossing the street and sees a big car heading directly towards him at high speed. If his brain does not know the truth – that the impact of a car travelling at 100 miles per hour will have certain unpleasant effects on the human body – what will it do? It will make no effort to avoid the car.

The brain needs to know the truth to survive. The more accurate the information in its mental data bank, the greater the possibility of survival.

This is why most people are uneasy when they lie. At a deep level, your brain knows that by lying, it may be threatening its own survival and that of others.

Dr Paul Brown, a noted psychologist in the United States, has studied the characteristics of successful leaders, coaches and managers for more than twenty years. His analysis has revealed that the primary characteristic

BrainSmart!

Use the following methods to maximize the benefits of your truth-seeking brain:

- When someone shares new information with you, note the process your brain goes through to evaluate its accuracy.
- Have you ever said, 'That's not fair!' This feeling is triggered by your truth-seeking brain. Listen to the number of times your work associates describe business situations with this phrase. What are your thoughts when you hear this phrase?
- Check the current validity of your fundamental beliefs.
- Gather and validate information in a new situation, or an old one that feels uncomfortable.

people look for in their leaders is trustworthiness: 'Can I trust/believe what this person is telling me?'

When people believe that the commitments made during a meeting will be honoured, they are much more likely to take action. But violation of trust always has serious consequences in a relationship. Who wants to be lied to? 'Give it to me straight' is how many people phrase it. Integrity is an extremely important characteristic for becoming successful.

As our brain edits its inputs, it constantly evaluates the new data using this criterion: 'Can I believe this, or is it garbage?' Once the brain decides to accept the new data as valid, synergy combines this with existing knowledge to trigger new thoughts and ideas.

One of the problems we frequently encounter is that people do not judge data accurately, or they have beliefs and ideas with little basis in fact, or they fail to update themselves. Many times, the question 'When did you first acquire that belief?' evokes the response, 'Well, twenty years ago . . .' or 'When I was in school . . .'. The appropriateness of the information has never been re-evaluated, to see if it still applies.

Brain Principle 7: The brain is persistent

One of the brain's most important attributes is its ability to persist, to continue striving for success no matter what the odds. The brain, using its synergistic, creative skills, will continue generating ideas and plans, in order to reach the goal. However, it is vital to focus on the defined goal, not the obstacles.

Any time our brain learns a new skill or creates a new thought, substantial effort is required in the initial attempt. Imagine an explorer hacking a pathway through a dense tropical jungle. The journey is the most difficult the first time. Each subsequent trip down the pathway becomes easier until, after many journeys, little effort is required.

Our brain works in a similar fashion. Having a thought for the first time is the most difficult. Each subsequent time we have the same thought, we make it easier to have the same thought again. The more often we have a thought, the more likely we are to have the identical thought in the future.

The implication of this pattern is that the brain naturally persists towards a goal that is in focus. When it stops persisting, we should question our commitment to reaching the goal.

When striving to accomplish a difficult goal, there is normally a moment of truth. Our first attempts may result in failure, leading us to question our ability to succeed. In his book *Learned Optimism*, Dr Martin Seligman explores the importance of persistence.

When people feel helpless and believe that a problem is both pervasive and permanent, they tend to give up trying to resolve it. However, unlike many adults, infants do not dwell on the concept of 'failure'. They are preoccupied with the desired goal, the finished product. They do not bombard themselves with negative self-talk, such as 'I can't do this!' or 'I'm so clumsy/stupid/awful!' Their brains' natural persistence allows them to keep working until they achieve what they want.

Keep this in mind the next time you are trying to do something difficult. If your first reaction when you hit a snag is to flood your mind with negative self-talk, modify it to be more confident and persistent: work in a brain-friendly fashion. With your amazing brain at the helm, knowing how to steer, you can only succeed.

Summary of the Brain Principles: The brain is naturally creative

The brain links and associates new ideas and sensory inputs with its existing knowledge and experience base. Every new input is connected to your

BrainSmart!

Use these methods to maximize the benefits of persistence:

- Read the biographies of famous people you admire. You may be amazed to learn about the setbacks/failures/discouragements they overcame on the way to success.
- Find a few people you trust to support you in your progress towards an important goal. Ask for their assistance in keeping you focused on achieving the goal. Look to them for encouragement when you doubt your chances of success.
- The next time you are learning a new skill, monitor your self-talk. Distinguish between positive, neutral and negative statements. Does your self-talk need adjustment?

core knowledge, and builds upon it. This synergistic linking of new ideas to existing knowledge is the engine's fuel for persistence. All these factors contribute to success when a clearly defined goal is established. Creative people take advantage of this linking and associating power by encouraging dialogue with others. They learn everything possible about issues that matter, and create an environment which encourages and nurtures ideas during the formative and developmental stages. Mimicking and benchmarking are used in a positive way to feed knowledge into the bio-computer.

You have a capacity for creativity that is beyond anything you could imagine. Challenge your truth-seeking brain by trying different experiences. Remember these seven Brain Principles, and check your actions and results against each of them.

Leadership profile: Pastor Tom Berninger

Pastor Tom Berninger first heard about the seven Brain Principles after he had attended one of our effective leadership seminars. We realized that at the heart of his pastor's approach to leadership were the seven Brain Principles; however, his source was so impeccable that it was impossible to ignore.

'I learned most of the seven Brain Principles by studying the life of Jesus and the Bible,' said Tom, Pastor of the Lincoln Park Abundant Life

Worship Center in Lincoln Park, New Jersey. 'For example, when Jesus fed the multitudes, he didn't do it all by himself. He broke the masses into groups, and delegated his disciples to work with the groups.'

Since 1981, Tom has been either a youth pastor or a church pastor – demanding jobs which require the ability to lead and inspire. Tom didn't know much about such matters when he began, but it didn't take him long to discover that good workers and leaders aren't born – they are made. Even those with the greatest desire to excel still need a vision and a sense of direction.

When he was put in charge of the youth programme a few years ago, he quickly learned that his leaders needed the desire and ability to work together as a team – not as individuals – for the ultimate benefit of everyone. 'One lone ranger could disrupt the team chemistry necessary for success,' he said. 'Though I encouraged individual expression, each individual still had to be part of the flow of the whole team.'

By applying the seven Brain Principles, Tom has helped create many generations of leaders whose work has been of such a high standard that the Church and its programmes have grown phenomenally.

In fewer than six years, Pastor Tom's flock grew from one youth leader and 30 kids to five youth leaders and 200 kids, while at the same time his Church grew from 200 members to 1 000!

Here, in his own words, Tom explains some of the ways he has applied the seven Brain Principles.

BRAIN PRINCIPLE 1: THE BRAIN SYNERGIZES INFORMATION SO THAT 1 PLUS 1 IS 2 OR MORE

> Being creative was an important part of our children's ministry. New ideas become old very quickly. It was impossible for me to come up with all the ideas for the groups myself. Believe me, I tried. I began requiring each leader to bring to each meeting a list of new ideas to be discussed by the team. This team discussion always led to the creation of even more ideas. For example, an older group of kids might be holding a treasure hunt in their cars. This might prompt an idea by the leader of a younger group to organize a treasure hunt, too, on church property.

BRAIN PRINCIPLE 2: THE BRAIN IS A SUCCESS-DRIVEN MECHANISM

At one time it was common to go month after month discussing the same idea, yet never seeing it come to fruition. When nothing was ever successfully completed, everyone was frustrated.

The problem was that people tend to procrastinate because they don't have a clear plan. I learned that they needed to write down the goals and their details or they never get on track towards accomplishing them. After a lot of frustration on my part I implemented what I call the ACBD technique:

A: Know where you are.
C: Determine where you want to be.
B: Know what you have to do to get from A to C
D: Do it!

Normally, if you give someone an assignment to be completed by Saturday, the average person wouldn't start thinking about it until Friday. Then they spend the last day working out the details and dealing with the unexpected. By Saturday afternoon, they're going crazy. So right at the planning table I started having them write down on their calendar on what day and at what time during the week they were going to work on the project. I asked, 'Do you need any help? If so, who is going to help you? Do you need anything purchased? If so, what?' In ten minutes, 75 per cent of the project planning was completed and they had an outline of what they needed to do. It made the path clearer, and things got done better and faster.

BRAIN PRINCIPLE 3: THE BRAIN HAS THE ABILITY TO MIMIC ACTIONS PERFECTLY

I never liked the idea of 'Do as I say, not as I do.' I believe in setting the best example I can because those under me will pick up cues from my own behaviour. As the youth pastor, I arrived for meetings early and was the last to leave. I never took advantage of my position. The unspoken message was, 'If I can get here early, so can you.' I would set up chairs and sweep floors. This taught my leaders that what we did was a team effort. They began to mimic my attitude, my enthusiasm and my work ethic because they believed in me, and began learning to do things they had never done before, simply by watching me. My directors would then encourage their leaders to mimic them, and soon the kids began to unconsciously take on the characteristics of the leaders.

BRAIN PRINCIPLE 4: THE BRAIN CRAVES COMPLETENESS – IT NEEDS TO FILL IN THE BLANKS

I've seen this phenomenon many times when what was expected of someone wasn't carefully spelled out. What I wanted them to do and what they thought I wanted them to do often didn't match. To demonstrate how easy it is to misunderstand, I set a bottle on the table in front of me and told people to describe it. Then I described it from my perspective. Even though we were looking at the same bottle, my description was different from theirs because I was looking at the back and they were looking at the front. When I counselled people or had meetings, I made sure things were clearly stated with no room for misinterpretation. I not only said, 'This project needs to be completed by Saturday,' but they also knew the time, what the project entailed and what steps were required for completion.

Sometimes we leave too much to the imagination. If you want specific things done in a specific way, you have to be specific and require those under you to tell you what you just told them. If you don't do this, people will come up with 1 001 excuses why it wasn't done right or wasn't done on time.

We have to be careful to communicate our thoughts with completeness. Too often, people use what I call 'crystal ball communication'. This communication pattern usually relies on the wrong assumption that the other person knows what I'm talking about. When I'm trying to relay an idea, I try to use words to paint a picture in the mind of the listener.

We've all played the game of 'telephone' when we were younger, where a statement is passed down a line of children, and when it reaches the end it barely resembles the original phrase. This often happens in adult communication as well.

What is really dangerous is that the more uncomfortable a topic is to discuss, the more we rely on 'crystal ball communication'.

Unfortunately, the more uncomfortable or sensitive the topic is, the more important clarity and completeness is.

BRAIN PRINCIPLE 5: THE BRAIN CONSTANTLY SEEKS NEW KNOWLEDGE AND INFORMATION

It was my job to help maintain the vitality in the leadership and therefore in the ministry. The way I did this was to mentally challenge my leaders. I routinely taught them something new. Each monthly meeting started with a five- to ten-minute lesson designed to make sure the leaders didn't fall into a rut. Second, I turned to outside sources, such as articles relevant to the goals of our ministry, that I would pass out and recommend they read. Third, there was a constant push to create. My directors and leaders were required to regularly develop different activities to keep them mentally fit and to always keep the children on their toes.

My motto was to stay on the cutting edge.

BRAIN PRINCIPLE 6: THE BRAIN IS TRUTH-SEEKING

This principle couldn't be more evident than in a church environment. If there were a loss of trust, there would be a loss of everything we stood for and therefore a loss of purpose. This had to start with me, and filter out to all. Trust and truthfulness are extremely important. You can't be an effective leader without it. People who don't trust you will be unwilling to go that extra mile when necessary.

I held myself to the ultimate standard so that those under me would strive for the highest standard possible for themselves.

BRAIN PRINCIPLE 7: THE BRAIN IS PERSISTENT

It is a natural tendency of most people to quit when they feel challenged, or to set goals for themselves far lower than their potential. Almost every director or leader under me at one time came to me and said, 'I can't do that,' or 'It's easy for you because it's natural for you.'

It became my job to turn on the switch of the seventh Brain Principle. I would not let them quit or take the easy way out.

After a while, they were learning to do things they never felt capable of. I reminded people that you may not be able to lift 200 pounds the first time you try, but as you train, you increase your capacity to lift. The same goes for your other abilities.

One young woman told me she wanted to quit because she simply could not stand up in front of a roomful of people and speak. I worked with her and encouraged her, and after six months she was doing all those things she thought she couldn't do. My directors were, of course, required to pass this attitude on until it touched the children we were trying to reach.

RESULTS

The benchmark here is the quality – and quantity – of leaders turned out by Pastor Tom's understanding of how the brain excels. Although in a Church the size of his there are many different pools from which to choose leaders to run or manage the many different ministries, the vast majority chosen have come though the training in the youth department. This pool has produced four associate pastors, three of whom have been sent out to start their own Churches, 14 out of 16 elders, the head of the Sunday school department, the children's ministry, choir, music ministry, ushers and the arts department.

'These people are all products of the training they received while working in the youth ministry,' said Pastor Tom. 'The loudest cheer to be heard in favour of any method or principle is the success that the Brain Principles have produced.'

Conclusion

There are seven Brain Principles covered in this chapter plus the good news that you have a limitless capacity to create. Being aware of these principles in your daily work will help you to achieve more from your magnificent brain as well as enjoy a better quality of life. Leaders need to fully understand and use the seven Brain Principles in their daily business life to achieve optimum results.

ACTIVITIES

1. Make a list of four of your favourite role models and ask yourself the following questions with regard to each.

   Role model's name

   What attracts me to this person?

   What can I learn from this person?

2. Starting tomorrow, have lunch-time conversations with people that are focused on helping you achieve your goals.

3. Write down three business goals that you want to achieve in the next month, and then three action steps you will take towards achieving each of these goals.

   Goal 1

   Action step 1

   Action step 2

   Action step 3

   Goal 2

   Action step 1

   Action step 2

Action step 3

Goal 3

Action step 1

Action step 2

Action step 3

4. **At the close of your next three conversations, once completed, check the other person's mental pictures by asking them to describe the conversation to you so it can be verified for accuracy.**

5. **At the next meeting you attend, note which Brain Principles are being used.**

   Meeting   **Date**

   Brain Principles:

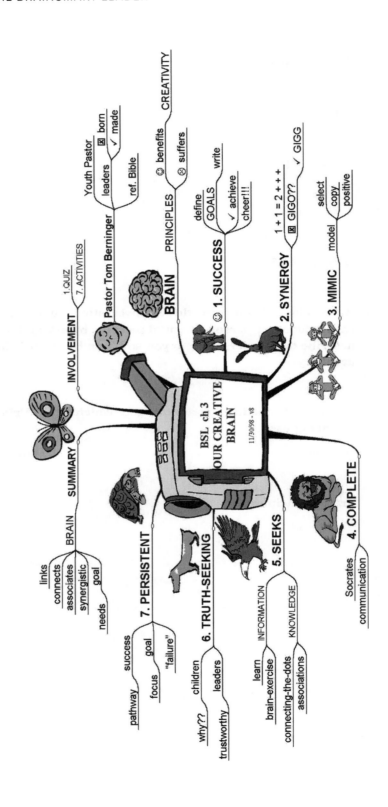

4 MIND MAPPING®

Quiz

1. Do you recognize the importance of colour in activating your brainpower?   Yes/No

2. In the natural process of thinking, is the brain using the right side at any given moment?   Yes/No

3. Can you easily link different ideas together?   Yes/No

4. Does using symbols in your notes and diaries indicate that you are bored with the subject in question?   Yes/No

5. Are you aware how mental pictures influence your thinking?   Yes/No

6. Do you draw pictures or doodle while speaking on the phone? Yes/No

7. Do you use pictures to facilitate your thinking process?   Yes/No

8. Do you understand how to use colour in developing your memory?   Yes/No

9. Do you have a tool for clearly documenting customer requirements?   Yes/No

10. Are you able to remember information about people you meet?   Yes/No

SCORING

Score two points for each 'Yes', except question 4 which scores two points for 'No'.

If you scored 18 or more, then you have gained insights into how to use your creative brain in unique and powerful ways! A score of less than 18 means this chapter will result in a whole new way of thinking.

Overview

In this chapter, we will introduce you to a powerful graphic technique which provides a universal key to unlocking the potential of the brain – the Mind Map. This tool is applicable to every aspect of business where improved learning and thinking will enhance performance. We will show how to apply Mind Mapping techniques to your work and in your everyday life, whether making presentations, drawing up personal 'to do' lists, planning a sales strategy or clarifying your company's vision statement.

Cortical skills

Your brain receives information, sorts and stores it, processes it and communicates it.

When you talk to someone, they receive information from you using all their senses, which help them understand and store what is interpreted as relevant. To understand this process, you need to be familiar with how the brain works.

Research by Dr Robert Ornstein of the University of California, based on the Nobel prize-winning work of Dr Roger Sperry at the California Institute of Technology, has thrown more light on the different activities handled by each side of the brain. The brain has an inventory of thinking skills for processing, storing, and utilizing information, and for the creation of new ideas. The outer part of your brain (the cerebral cortex) is divided into two halves: the left and the right cortices.

The left cortex dominantly deals with:

- **Numbers**, which are used for costs and expenses measurements, and for keeping records.
- **Words**, which are used in communication, either verbal or written.
- **Logic**, which is involved in business decisions!
- **Lists**, which help keep track of, and give order to, the masses of information.
- **Details**, which help ensure that you create a complete picture, support an analysis or define specifications.

The right cortex dominantly deals with:

- **Pictures**, which are used in manuals and in verbally explaining situations.

- **Imagination,** which is used in thinking up new ideas for services or products.
- **Colour,** which can be used in packaging, graphs, charts and presentations.
- **Rhythm,** such as the rhythm of a conversation or buying cycles.
- **Space,** which has a variety of meanings; in building this could be the layout; in face-to-face meetings, it could be the arrangement of the seating.

Your brain doesn't use only one set of skills at a time, such as just the left-cortical skills or just the right-cortical skills. Its natural process when thinking or learning is to draw on skills from both sides of the cortex. Recent research shows that children who take classes which emphasize right-cortical skills (such as music and art lessons) perform better in classes which emphasize left-cortical skills (such as languages and mathematics). To maximize your creative powers, you must develop both sides of your brain!

MIND MATRIX

Complete the mind matrix in Figure 4.1, considering each of your ten mental skills, one at a time. First, ask yourself: 'How aware am I of the use of *numbers* when I'm in meetings or on the telephone?' If you think about 50 per cent, shade in the area up to 50 per cent, and write

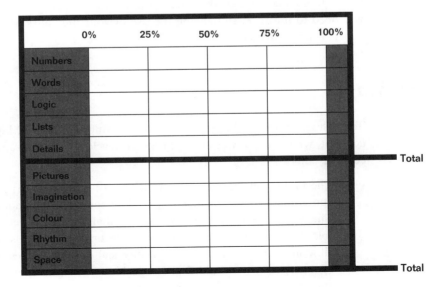

Figure 4.1 Mind matrix

BrainSmart!

We all have a natural stock of these basic cortical skills. Even if you have not fully developed all these skills, you can do so once you decide that you want to.

Creativity requires the integration of all cortical skills. If you do not consider yourself to be creative, work on improving those cortical skills which you think are your weakest. Expect a surge of ideas!

in '50' in the right-hand shaded column. Repeat the process for each of the cortical skills.

Now add your scores for the first five mental skills, from *numbers* to *details*. Write the total score on the 'Total' line at the bottom of the section.

Next, add your scores for the remaining mental skills, from *pictures* to *space*. Write down the total score on the 'Total' line at the bottom of that section.

How did you do? If you have equally shaded the top set (the left cortical mental skills) and the bottom set (the right cortical mental skills), you are using a whole creative brain approach. But if one set has a higher score and is more shaded than the other, you can immediately see which areas you need to improve. Enhancing the use of your mental skills will result in superior performance and a naturally creative brain.

Mind Maps®

Tony Buzan explains the genesis of his revolutionary Mind Mapping concept, which is one way to explore and develop your full range of cortical skills.

> The first significant step occurred when I was 14. I was given numerous tests on intelligence, reading speed and memory. The results were poor, and I was told that I would never be able to change the results. As well as infuriating me, this was difficult to understand. After all, physical exercise makes you stronger, so why shouldn't the right kind of mental exercise improve your mental performance, too? I immediately began to work on this problem with the firm belief that if I could devise

the right technique, my results would surely improve. It was at this stage that I also realized that the least productive method of trying to understand a subject was to take the kind of notes that students had been taking for centuries. I found them boring and worthless, and the more I took, the less I seemed to understand the material. For the next six years I contemplated a variety of non-traditional study techniques, none of which satisfied me.

At age 20, while I was studying at the University of British Columbia, I began to work seriously on improving my memory and note-taking.

First, I studied the nature of memory, and especially that which is recalled. This inevitably includes imagery, association and location.

Second, I studied the note-taking methods of the great brains, and observed that, without exception, they all used images, pictures, arrows and other connective devices.

The result of this combined study was the evolution, in 1969, of the concept of Mind Mapping, which ultimately became part of memory/learning/thinking systems I called 'Mental Literacy.' The more I uncovered, the more excited I became. I felt like the discoverers of Tutankhamun's tomb. First of all, I had peered through a keyhole and seen the vague shapes of what might be fantastic artifacts. Then I had entered the barely lit room and witnessed the astonishing potential of its contents. Next, I had managed to cast light on the wealth of treasure I had discovered. Finally, they were not only mine, but could be shared with everyone (and became greater as the wealth was shared).

I wanted very much to tell the world about my discovery, and I still do. The first communication of it came with the publication in 1974 of my book *Use Your Head* and the BBC television series of the same name, which was repeated every year for ten years. Disseminating the idea involved twenty-five years of world-wide travelling on lecture tours to academic, business and government institutions. Then, at the beginning of the 1990s, came the establishment by Vanda North of the Buzan Centres, where instructors are trained and licensed in

Mental Literacy. The Mind Map process provides a brain-friendly note-taking system that also facilitates recall. The two areas of study came together, synergetically.

HOW TO MIND MAP

Now it's your turn to Mind Map! Learn this simple technique, and delight in how quickly you can apply it to benefit yourself, both professionally and personally. Look at Figure 4.2, and then follow these instructions:

1. Gather a selection of coloured pens or pencils.
2. Take a large white sheet of paper (standard A4 or quarto will do) and place it with the longer axis horizontal.
3. Select the topic, problem or subject to be Mind Mapped – this will be the basis of your central image.
4. Gather any materials, research or additional information that is needed, so that you have all the facts at your fingertips.
5. Now start to draw in the centre of your page with an image approximately 10cm (2 inches) square. Choose a word or image that represents the main idea you want to capture. For example, if you've thought of putting on a Las Vegas theme party to enthuse your staff about taking a chance with a new programme, the image could be a slot machine.
6. Use dimension, expression and at least three colours in the central image in order to attract your attention and aid memory.
7. Make the branches that are closest to the centre thick, attached to the image and 'organic' (wavy). These branches hold the sub-topics, for example 'date', 'catering', 'attire', 'speeches' would be relevant to the Las Vegas theme party (see Figure 4.3). Branches should be no longer than the space it takes to print the word or draw the image. Draw branches for every idea related to the party, and print a single word on each of those branches.
8. Branch thinner lines off the end of the appropriate branch to hold supporting data.
9. Use images wherever possible. You do not need to be a good artist, this is simply a way to enhance retention and enjoyment of the material.
10. Use colours as your own special code to show people, topics, themes, dates, and to make your Mind Map more attractive.
11. Capture all your ideas, or those that others have contributed, then edit, reorganize, beautify, elaborate or clarify as a second and more advanced stage of thinking.

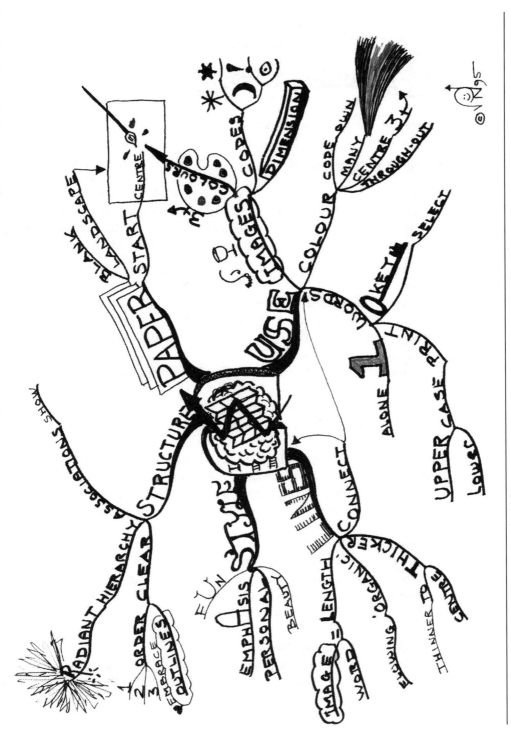

Figure 4.2 A Mind Map on How to Mind Map

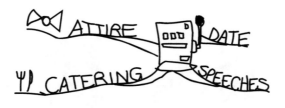

Figure 4.3 Las Vegas theme party

MIND MAP BENEFITS

A Mind Map harnesses the full range of cortical skills – words, imagination, numbers, logic, rhythm, pictures, lists, details, colour and space – in a single, uniquely powerful manner. In so doing, it gives you the freedom to roam the infinite expanses of your brain. Like a road map, a Mind Map will:

- give you a quick, one-page overview of a large subject/area/problem/topic
- enable you to plan strategy/make choices
- let you know where you are going, and where you have been
- gather and hold large amounts of data on one page and see the links and gaps
- encourage both daydreaming and problem-solving by exploring creative pathways
- allow you to be extremely efficient
- be enjoyable to look at, read, muse over and remember.

Mind Maps have many applications, as we shall soon discover. In particular, you now have the perfect tool with which to capture information, retain it in your long-term memory, and reproduce it in Mind Map form for clarification of thinking or effective communication.

For instance, if you are interested in computers and read journals on the subject, there will be many publications which you think are valuable, but too much information to commit to memory. There is a method you can use to capture every bit of data from those journals you consider significant and have it at your fingertips at a glance.

A Magazine Mind Map Book

Create a Mind Map book by placing blank paper into a binder or use a Mind Map pad. In this case, you would dedicate one of the pages to a computer magazine. When the magazine arrives, here's what to do:

1. Read it as you normally would, marking items of interest.

Figure 4.4 Magazine Mind Map book

2. Draw a picture of the magazine or a computer in the centre of your Mind Map.
3. Mind Map the complete magazine. This will enable you to remember the items of interest.
4. Now go through the publication again, this time reading in depth the items that interest you, and Mind Map these ideas as separate branches. For example, if one article were on the Internet, one branch would say 'Internet'. Another branch might be 'hard-drive' or 'software', and off that 'accounting' (see Figure 4.4). Remember that you can put all the key ideas from this magazine down on the one page. The same rules of Mind Mapping covered in this chapter apply to your Magazine Mind Map. Where you have a magazine that is very important, we suggest that you choose articles in which you have a particular interest, and Mind Map them separately. This enables you to develop more detailed Mind Maps of important subjects for future reference and study.
5. You will notice that some items in the magazine are connected to each other. For example, an article on Internet security may be linked to another story because it covers modems. To show this linkage, use a distinct handwriting style on each of these branches, use the same colour-code, or use a common icon or symbol.
6. When you have finished the magazine, scan it again to make sure you have not missed anything.
7. Take your one-page overview Mind Map and display it at home or at work in a place where you can see and review it easily. Any time you generate an idea related to one of these magazine articles, add it to your Mind Map. Be aware that 80 per cent of what you read will be forgotten in 24 hours unless you review the material. Most people will forget everything they've read in a few days. You, however, will become and remain an expert because of the daily review of your Mind Map.
8. For the next two months, repeat the Mind Map process with your trade magazines. After three months, consolidate the Mind Maps from one magazine onto one new master Mind Map. Soon, you'll have more knowledge of your products than most!

Once you have developed a series of Mind Maps and reviewed them, you will be well on the way to building your knowledge base. You will make connections and associations with all this new material and it will become an important source of creative thinking.

BUSINESS APPLICATIONS

We normally take notes when something is so important that we want to remember it, or when we want to organize our thoughts, to plan, solve problems or set down ideas. When we use a Mind Map, we can do these things more quickly and more efficiently. Mind Mapping in a business environment can save time, help organize thinking and improve your ability to generate new ideas.

Phone Calls

Do you take notes during phone calls? With a Mind Map, you start with your central image, recording the date and the name of the person you are talking to. Start a new branch for each new subject, stemming from your central image. To add details, use one word per line, with each new line radiating from the main branches. This way of organizing information helps the brain remember, compare and connect very quickly. When the subject changes, add another branch, using key words on the lines.

If the other person returns to a previous subject, you simply return to that branch and add the new information. Colour adds another dimension: for example, red might signify actions to take immediately, green might indicate actions to take later. You can return to the same branch repeatedly to add additional facts. Information gathered by phone is often jumbled, but the Mind Map will place it in order when added to the appropriate branch. When you have finished the conversation, fold and store the Mind Map in a binder, placing the date and the caller's name in the top right-hand corner.

When you have another conversation with that person, refer to your original Mind Map, adding new branches on the same page for additional topics. You can fit a large amount of information on your one-page Mind Map over time: everything you have ever talked about with that person will be summarized on one page!

Presentations

Presentations can be planned in advance, with the main branches of the Mind Map representing each part of the presentation. You can set down as much detail as necessary, because key words and pictures condense the information.

With a Mind Map, you can take in the whole picture all the time, allowing you to see links, connections and associations within the presentation that otherwise might not have been apparent. A simple glance at the Mind Map as you are speaking, and you will find that each word or image triggers off a flow of thoughts and corresponding words. The audience will be under the impression that you are speaking without any notes at all!

Problem-Solving

How to increase sales and how to find new customers are two problems constantly addressed. Using Mind Maps will help you discover the answers. Start with a central image that represents the problem you're addressing, for example, if the question relates to ways of increasing sales, you could use a sack of money.

Next, draw three branches, one named PLUSES, the next MINUSES and the last INTERESTING. Note all the positive ideas first on the PLUSES branch, no matter how stupid or silly they may seem, because they may lead to creative breakthroughs later on. Next, complete the MINUSES branch, and finally the INTERESTING branch. Work as fast as you can – your Mind Map may look messy, but the ideas you generate may well surprise you!

Generating Ideas (Mentally Literate Brainstorming)

One important use of Mind Maps is to generate ideas. This technique resembles brainstorming with a group, but you can carry it out on your own – we will refer to it as 'brain blooming'. Start with a central image of the outcome you want: for example, you may wish to improve the performance of your team. The central image could be a picture of happy people. As ideas flow, make and add branches. Writing down key words that represent ideas you have already had can trigger additional related thoughts that result in creative breakthroughs. For the next steps refer to the Group Mind Map section p. 62.

Planning Meetings

Do you spend a good deal of time preparing for meetings? Mind Maps will help you prepare both rapidly and accurately.

Drawing the main branches of topics to be covered beforehand will help to clarify your ideas.

Attending Meetings

Do you take notes when attending meetings? If so, what do your notes look like? One of the problems you have probably faced is that people usually speak much faster than you can write!

A Mind Map gives you a structure for collecting information in an orderly fashion, even though it may come in bits and pieces. You can colour-code who is speaking, as well as the important ideas and actions to be taken. The Mind Map can capture it all – the information and an action plan – on the same page.

Job Interviews

Do you have to interview and select staff? If so, a Mind Map can serve as a fast and accurate method of conducting future interviews.

Prepare a Mind Map format which can be used with any job applicant. Draw a central image representing the applicant. Branches might be labelled 'qualifications', 'personality', 'job history' and 'interests'. Colour can be used to show objective information in cool tones and subjective in warm tones. Make colour copies of this template Mind Map, and fill it in as you conduct the interview. You will be surprised both at the clarity of the resulting profile of each applicant and how much information you can take in at a glance!

Planning

Using a Mind Map for planning allows you to view the whole picture quickly. Everything you do relates to everything else you do, and this becomes apparent on the Mind Map. Are there any missing pieces? Do you need to juggle your resources? The Mind Map will immediately help you see what needs doing.

Reading Books

Next time you read an important book, Mind Map it. Once you have established a strong central image, study the table of contents, drawing a branch for each topic. As you read the book, add to the chapter branches of the Mind Map, even if you don't read the chapters in order.

THE GROUP MIND MAP

An invaluable application for a manager is a Group Mind Map, which can be used to solicit ideas, to highlight differences and similarities, and to make sure everyone is working towards a common purpose.

Begin by asking members of the group to individually Mind Map the theme. Then note the differences in the words used and the similarity of themes. Construct a small Group Mind Map showing the Basic Ordering Ideas (the equivalent of chapter titles in a book). Finally, go through the same process on a large piece of paper, drawing up the Group Mind Map, collecting everyone's ideas on a series of branches. When the Mind Map is complete, you will have a more cohesive team with greater understanding of the situation, and all the individuals involved will be oriented in the same direction. Nobody will be left out, and everybody has contributed and can see the full picture. This use of Mind Mapping improves the chance of securing commitment from all the team members.

Mind Map Example: Sandy Hahn, IBM

Sandy Hahn is IBM's Manager of International Assignment Change Integration. This is what she says about Mind Mapping:

> We have been using Mind Maps with work groups to facilitate the creative process of their brains. The results they are producing have shown us that Mind Maps can be the link from continuous improvement to re-engineering.
>
> When a team of people start Mind Mapping an issue or broken process, they create a clear picture of what is actually going on or not going on, with appropriate links and connections. This encourages and enables the brains of the participants to begin creating alternatives for attaining the goal of the process.
>
> Here is an example from our consulting work. At IBM, a human resource and an accounting team got together to try to improve their payment system for language lessons for international assignees. They Mind Mapped the current process, looking for the areas most in need of change. When they completed the Mind Map, many members of the integrated team saw a new picture they had never recognized before. This became the catalyst to research the true requirements of the customers of the process. From that point it became easier to understand the current activities related to meeting those requirements – from suppliers, through the firm, to the ultimate customer. Seeking feedback from customers and process participants on how well the process was performing allowed the team to identify and prioritize problems and gaps. That led them to create various alternatives to test with customers across the firm's key functions. The

team finished its work by generating solutions, which resulted in a radical redesign of their workflow, an 80 per cent reduction in costs, and a 70 per cent reduction in the time it took to pay for lessons. An entire accounts payable system was eliminated, paperwork was reduced significantly, and reconciliations were automated, leading to increased customer satisfaction and reduced workload.

Sandy is delighted with the results of her team's efforts: 'Mind Mapping alleviated the frustration of a complex process which spans over sixty countries. Feedback from the customer and our "new tool" assured us we were on the right track.'

A leadership profile of Sandy Hahn can be found in Chapter 7.

Leadership profile: Tiger Vessels

Tiger Vessels is CEO of Union Transport, a freight forwarding company headquartered in Johannesburg, South Africa.

Tiger Vessels and two associates founded Union Transport with $10 000 in 1978. The three had met while working for a large freight forwarding company which didn't have the kind of vision about the industry that Tiger and his partners believed was necessary to sustain success. Tiger believed you couldn't just have contract people in other countries operating on your behalf, but needed to have your own offices there. It would not be an easy road. Their first international venture, in the USA, failed, but the trio (which has since become a quartet) persisted.

Union Transport has grown from six employees in 1978 to 5 000 employees in 172 offices in 32 countries with revenues of $500 million. The company's objective for the year 2000 is revenues of $1 billion. Union Transport is listed on the Johannesburg Stock Exchange.

Why has Union Transport not only survived but beaten the odds, to experience phenomenal growth and success? It has much to do with Tiger Vessels' leadership. Tiger is the quintessential BrainSmart Leader, who knows how to stimulate employees' creativity and encourage a synergy within his organization that energizes and perpetuates itself.

'At the top of our management, we have what we call an "umbrella vision",'

Tiger explains. The leaders have a vision about where they want to go. They communicate this to their staff, but leave it up to them to achieve it however they see fit. 'We allow each part of the organization to build its own vision, so that whatever ideas they come up with are more powerful and more likely to succeed,' he says. 'Because the ideas are theirs and not ours, they feel empowered.'

Tiger never forgets that those who work for him are people, not machines. He sees each person as a valuable individual, and takes great pains to treat them as such: 'I spend a great deal of one-on-one time with people in my organization,' he says. 'My door is always open, and I make sure to ask whether they have personal problems they need to discuss. People need to get that sort of thing off their chest before they can have a fruitful session relating to business. If that's all we talk about, that's fine. I give the senior executives an hour and a half. I never want them to feel that I'm rushing them.'

Tiger and his partners, who call themselves 'associates', don't stay in an ivory tower while the peons below toil. As a result, they know everything that is going on, and are more involved in problem-solving.

'People say you can't be a manager if you're involved in day-to-day activities, but we feel quite the opposite,' Tiger explains. 'Because we *are* involved, when things go wrong the guys actually call us to come in and help. This is fantastic, and better for everyone than a situation where you just sit there trying to control other people.'

Other things are done differently at Union Transport, too. Whenever people come up with a creative idea, they jot it down in the company's 'sales bible', in case it could be useful in the present or might be useful in the future. If it's found to be useful, a training module may be developed around that particular idea.

'I want people to be introspective about the way they operate,' Tiger says. 'The bible encourages them to say, "This could work and others can benefit from it." That way, the organization is learning from itself and isn't relying on a handful of guys to produce all the new stuff. That's why I encourage all the salespeople and managers to keep journals: "This happened – what I should have done was x." The mere process of documenting a thought or action reinforces their ideas and helps them to start thinking critically about the growth process. Without exception, every person who applies what we teach them, grows. That growth helps ideas bubble up from inside the organization.'

Tiger and all his sales force see a minimum of five customers a week. Tiger discourages salespeople from making sales appointments before 10.30 a.m., even though their workday starts at 8 a.m. He wants them to have two and a half hours to just think about their business and handle administrative tasks. 'If you discipline yourself that way, it works. People who start their appointments at 8 a.m. end up with such a full day they don't have time to think and reflect,' Tiger explains, 'and you need that thinking time.'

Mind Mapping is another tool used at Union Transport, which has enhanced creativity, planning, learning and documenting ideas. 'I learned about Mind Mapping twenty years ago,' says Tiger. 'It struck me as such a simple technique. I had always had difficulty structuring my thoughts as a student. The fact that thoughts are not linear but are all over the place and could be organized by Mind Mapping struck me as common sense. Now, we hardly go to a meeting where someone isn't Mind Mapping what's going on. I don't know how I would have managed without Mind Mapping. Many of our staff feel the same way.'

Tiger uses Mind Mapping to plan speeches and presentations to customers. He Mind Maps customers' needs, he uses them when planning proposals, to minute meetings, and during think-tank sessions to keep track of and stimulate ideas. He saves all his Mind Maps in notebooks that go back many years. His employees share Mind Maps, and display some of them on the walls, so others can contribute ideas.

Like any other company, Union Transport has had its share of ups and downs, but the bad times have been weathered successfully thanks to the approach its leaders have taken to the problems.

'Much of our growth happened during times of adversity,' Tiger says. 'I honestly believe that if you start from an optimistic outlook, your chances of getting where you want to go are a lot better. We've had a variety of real disasters come our way, but we've faced them, asked ourselves what we were going to do about it, planned diligently, and portrayed a sense of confidence to those around us – and it's worked.'

His philosophy has yielded another sort of success for Tiger, too. Although he has more money than he could ever spend, he chooses to live a modest life, devoid of fancy cars and homes: 'Of course I enjoy a healthy bottom line, but what really turns me on is seeing the people around me grow. When I see a young man who joined us as a dispatch rider become a general manager, that gives me a huge kick. I enjoy being a catalyst that helps others grow.'

Conclusion

The potential applications for Mind Maps are endless. You can use them to study any topic, revise for exams, see the 'big picture' in any situation, memorize, organize personal and professional events, and to prepare for negotiations.

ACTIVITIES

Here is a series of activities to assist you in developing your Mind Map skills. According to Tony Buzan, you need to produce at least 100 Mind Maps to understand the full range of possibilities and to have created a new habit.

1. Create a Mind Map of your future career.

2. Create a Mind Map of a book, operating manual or job description you need to know about.

3. Create a Mind Map of the next workshop or seminar you attend.

4. Create a Mind Map of the next customer (internal or external) meeting you have.

5. Create a Mind Map of a team or department meeting.

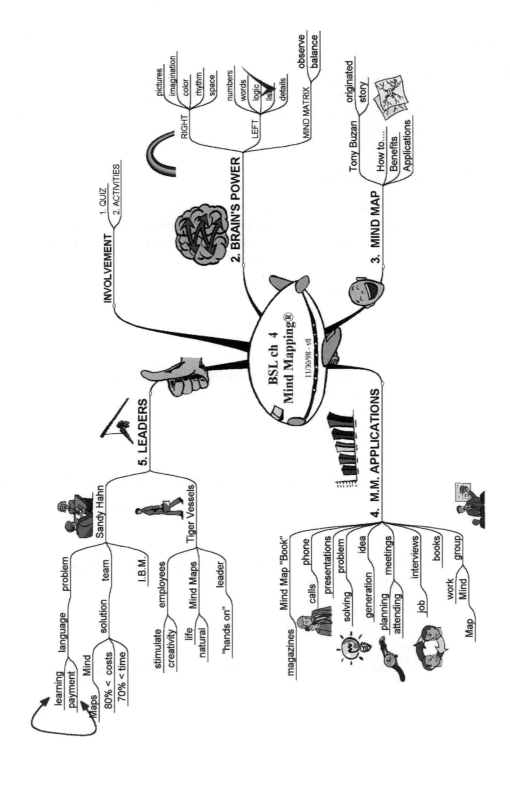

5 THE POWER OF THE VISION

Quiz

1. Do you know what you really want in your business or career? Yes/No

2. Can you describe a vision for yourself and/or your company?   Yes/No

3. Do you believe that you are a creative force in your life?   Yes/No

4. Do other people understand and support your vision?   Yes/No

5. Is your vision causing you to stretch and move out of
   your comfort zone?   Yes/No

6. Have you devised ways to constantly remind yourself of
   your vision, e.g. wall charts?   Yes/No

7. Do you have a series of goals or plans to assist you in
   reaching your vision?   Yes/No

8. Does your company have a vision that inspires its work force? Yes/No

9. Have you identified the critical factors that will help you
   reach your vision?   Yes/No

10. Are you willing to make sacrifices and persist until you reach
    your vision?   Yes/No

SCORING

Score two points for each Yes.
If you scored over 18 points, you have already developed a clear vision and understand how to use this vision to lead people. This chapter will reinforce your leadership skills. If you scored 18 or less, this chapter will show you how to create and communicate your vision.

Overview

This chapter covers the importance of both individual and corporate visions, explaining why a vision is effective, and how you can both construct and successfully implement a vision.

Vision power

If someone asks you what kind of future you want for yourself, are you likely to say, 'I want to be unhappy, insecure, confused and unsuccessful'? This may sound like a ridiculous notion, but it is what often awaits those who don't consciously envision their desired future. As we now understand from what we have learned about how our creative brain works, we need to give it precise direction to arrive at the desired destination. Another way of looking at this is what we term 'the complete picture'.

It is surprising how many companies lack a vision. This is as damaging to a company as to an individual. Both are entrusting their future to chance.

Warren Bennis talks of leadership development, saying that success during the information revolution depends on a corporation's ability to produce Intellectual Capital – 'consisting of know-how, expertise, brain power, innovation, and ideas promoted in an organizational environment that will not only be fast, focused, flexible and friendly, but also fun'.

He goes on to say that in future, the key to competitive advantage: 'will be the capacity of leaders to create the social architecture capable of generating Intellectual Capital'. All good CEOs tell me that their major challenge is, "How do I release the brain power of the people in my company?" '

A vision made real by Mental Literacy is designed to do just that.

Burt Nanus, in his book *Visionary Leadership* writes: 'There's no more powerful engine driving an organization towards excellence and long-range success than an attractive, worthwhile and achievable vision of the future, widely shared.'

A vision is an attractive future for you or your company which inspires your creative brain to help you achieve it. It gives you direction, helps keep you focused, stimulates your creativity, and challenges limiting beliefs.

In the 1960s, President John F. Kennedy inspired NASA with his vision of putting a man on the moon, and returning safely, resulting in one of the largest management and organizational challenges ever undertaken. Many sceptics at the time scoffed at the idea, but the vision energized NASA employees to meet the challenge.

The Disney vision, 'We create happiness', is an outstanding example of the power that three simple words can conjure up in the minds of both employees and customers.

It would be quite ludicrous for Disney to adopt a vision which stated. 'We create unhappiness', yet so many organizations do just that by default. With no vision, employees and management are doomed to mediocrity.

Peter M. Senge, author of *The Fifth Discipline*, says: 'Where there is genuine vision, people excel and learn, not because they are told to, but because they want to.'

There is often confusion about a vision. It is neither a mission statement nor a goal. A mission statement is a general philosophy of how to reach a goal, such as 'produce the best product possible.' A goal is a stated purpose, such as 'to reach £1 million in sales by 1 August'. Both must relate to the vision – the how and what.

A vision is an imagined, possible, desirable future that is both dynamic and evolving, able to unleash intellectual capital and creativity. It is designed to attract commitment as well as energize people. For example, 'No more shacks' is the vision of Habitat for Humanity, which builds homes for the needy at affordable prices with volunteer labour; 'Save the planet. Love All. Serve All' is the vision of the Hard Rock Cafe, and Tony Buzan's vision for his organization is 'to create a world of Mentally Literate Humans.'

Once you have a working vision, check to see if it makes sense to those to whom it will apply. You may need to adjust the vision to make sure it's acceptable.

Next, share with your staff, using whatever means possible (many companies have visions hidden away in filing cabinets, where they do absolutely no good). The secret is to make certain that it is communicated often, and your staff share your vision

A salesman made the drawing of his vision shown in Figure 5.1. It depicts

BrainSmart!

To create a vision, you must answer the question: 'What do I really want?' Reducing your answer to a simple concept is challenging, and must meet certain criteria:

- Do not condition your choices by adding qualifiers such as 'if' or 'when.'
- Be specific.
- Focus on the end result, not how to achieve it (your creative brain will solve that problem).
- Regardless of your current mood, seek the end result.
- Create freely without previous experiences dictating your choices.
- Choose what *you* want, not what someone else wants for you.
- Think what is possible. Do not limit what you want.

himself climbing a mountain, waving a flag of security after reaching the top. This simple drawing was then placed on the salesman's fridge, so that he would see it daily as he worked to his desired vision.

One way to make a vision memorable employs storytelling or the use of metaphors. When Robert M. Elliott was president of the Levitz Furniture Corporation, he used this method. He spoke of the company being an imaginary train proceeding along a winding, uphill track, with many tunnels ahead. For those who stayed on board, the train would eventually reach its destination – a profitable, successful company. It was a powerful vision, easy to comprehend and recall.

Here are some other vehicles for communicating a vision.

- letters
- newsletters
- audio tapes
- posters
- clothing
- symbols (logos)
- Mind Maps
- videos
- comics
- lapel badges.

The more of the five senses that are employed in this communication, the

Figure 5.1   A salesman's vision

more effective and memorable it will be. We tend to rely primarily on sight and sound. In the leadership profile of Bob Hughes later in this chapter, he used *Star Trek: The Next Generation* as a multi-sensory theme to motivate, instruct and align his employees with the company's vision of being the most advanced, efficient and modern payroll department in the universe.

Multi-sensory visions are powerful because information transmitted via three senses will be at least three times more likely to register and be remembered than information transmitted by just one sense.

Bob Hughes at IBM didn't just tell his people he wanted them to be more efficient. He let them symbolically *experience* improvement and success through the *Star Trek* metaphore. A galaxy of planets glowed from the ceiling. *Star Trek* theme music was played throughout the meeting. Cake topped with *Star Trek* figures was served. People wore *Star Trek* costumes and Spock ears, and were challenged to 'taste the success of Accounts Payable in the 21st century'.

In his book *The Vision*, Richard Israel uses the example of the sales team which had entered a competition with the first prize of a trip to Paris. To make this vision multi-sensory, the sales manager, Sandy Stone, placed a poster of the Eiffel Tower on the office wall with a photograph of all the sales team taken at a party. Next to the poster she placed a bottle of champagne, on which she tied a French silk scarf that had been dipped in French perfume. By engaging several of their senses, her sales team had a clearer vision of the prize – and won it!

What makes vision power work?

Imagine yourself walking down a crowded big-city street. Across six lanes of bumper-to-bumper traffic you notice a shop you need to visit. You are leaving tomorrow, so you must go to the shop today. It's pouring with rain, and crossing the traffic could be a life-threatening challenge, but the need to go to that shop presents an irresistible challenge to your brain.

Perhaps you could find a traffic light at the next block and be able to double back. Maybe you could risk walking through the cars, pausing at each lane until you can proceed to the next. Maybe you could find a police officer and ask for help crossing the road. You could look for an umbrella or wait for the rain to let up, or decide it's worth getting soaked. Your creative brain will investigate a number of possibilities, but sooner or later it will come upon a route and method you find acceptable, and will guide you to your destination.

Consider what is happening in your brain as you contemplate the maze of complications for the vision you seek to realize:

1. In your mind's eye, you see yourself there.
2. You tell yourself, 'One way or the other, I'm *going* to get there.'
3. You find the energy necessary to move you towards your visionary outcome.
4. Your creative brain works out a strategy of how to get you there, weighing a number of possibilities.

This simple analogy illustrates what makes vision power work. Provided you concentrate on an attractive future or vision and you know where you are now (your current situation, and what you have and don't have), your creative brain will create the strategy and find the energy necessary to deliver you to your destination.

BrainSmart!

This is what it takes for anyone to turn their vision into reality. Here are the steps:

- Develop a clear understanding of what you want.
- Create a mental picture of what you want in as much detail as possible.
- Summarize that picture in a short written sentence. If you cannot state your vision in 15 words or less, you need to reframe and refocus until you can. The vision should be more like a general philosophy than a set of goals.
- If your vision involves your company, ask peers for feedback about it; if your vision is for you personally, ask a friend.
- Communicate the vision in as many ways as you can. This not only informs others, but also reinforces it in your mind.
- Keep taking actions that move you towards the realization of your vision.

The challenge of visionary leadership

When you think about visionary leaders, who comes to mind – Thomas Edison, Henry Ford, Bill Gates, Winston Churchill, Martin Luther King, Eleanor Roosevelt, Billy Graham, Mother Theresa? No doubt, you have your own list.

Although in quite disparate walks of life, these famous people have one quality in common – a personal vision, which they were able to communicate not only to the people working for them, but also to the masses.

Our belief is that they not only possessed powerful visions, but also used their creative brains to achieve those visions despite the obstacles in their way. They were persistent, committed and sure of what they wanted.

Leadership profile: Bob Hughes, IBM

In 1991 Bob Hughes faced the biggest challenge of his career. Bob was a manager who was responsible for consolidating IBM's corporate travel and relocation expense accounting into one nationalized, central operation in Endicott, New York State. Prior to this centralization, the accounting departments were found scattered throughout the USA, requiring too many staff and generating too much expense.

The plant was on the verge of being downsized because of budget pressures, and workers were being laid off due to a fall in workload. Bob was charged with retraining as many employees as possible to work in his newly created, centralized travel and relocation expense accounting division.

Bob had in front of him a blank sheet of paper – no existing structure or employees – and a very small budget. To his new workers, he wasn't exactly offering paradise: their offices would be temporary structures in an off-site parking lot littered with surplus furniture. With his enthusiasm, Bob convinced four people to move from their comfortable offices in Southbury, Connecticut, to work in the parking lot in Endicott – a distance of more than 200 miles.

None of the other 70 workers he hired, other than four managers with accounting backgrounds, knew a thing about expense accounting. Some were warehouse workers, some were secretaries, and others were cafeteria or maintenance workers.

Bob's challenge was to forge this diverse group of individuals into a close-knit team dedicated to becoming the best accounting organization in the USA. Under his leadership, Bob's team achieved his goal, and over the next five years won the prestigious CFO Reach Award and the Hackett Best Practices Award.

'The only thing I looked for in the people I hired was attitude,' said Bob. 'If they had the right attitude, I figured I could teach them three principles that would guarantee success.' Those three principles were:

1. Control
2. Challenge
3. Connect

CONTROL

Bob taught his workers that they controlled everything that happened in their careers: who they worked for, how much money they made, and whether or not they came to work. He emphasized that continuing their education would give them more control over their future: the more new skills they learned, the more choices they had regarding jobs and salary.

Bob backed up his words with action, and made education a priority. He started classes in accounting, and gave team members two weeks of classroom teaching, followed by two weeks to apply the training in the work environment. He then scheduled two more weeks in the classroom, each time bringing everyone a little more up to speed. Each new class expanded the subject by building upon the previous material – it truly was 'learning as you go'. The momentum generated by this continual cycle of education and application was like a snowball rolling down a mountain, continuing to gain size and speed until it reached the bottom.

Because of Bob's belief that the knowledge of his people was his most valuable asset, he resisted pressure to minimize the cost of training. 'Whenever a budget cut came, I said, "We need to invest more, not less, in education" ', Bob explained. 'I did whatever I could to make the savings up someplace else. I kept raising the level of the lowest common denominator. By raising the level of each individual's knowledge, even if only by small amounts, the improvement became exponential. You take 74 people with this increase in knowledge, and the results become phenomenal.'

CHALLENGE

Bob wanted his people to see their new responsibilities as a challenge – a challenge to put a smile on their customers' faces.

'The single focus, minute-to-minute, hour-to-hour, was to ask, "Are we working towards our goal and delighting our customers?" ' said Bob. With this as the guiding principle, he did not need to supervise his 74 employees closely. Whenever any doubt crept in about what they should be doing, all they had to do was remind themselves of their goal, and they would find their way back on track. This was true whether their job was to open the mail or to deal with a problem by telephone.

CONNECT

The staff had to form bonds with one another and see themselves as one big unit that would benefit by the sum total of each person's small successes.

Frequent pats on the back were an integral part of Bob's success formula, delivered to everyone when they achieved small or large successes. 'We came up with ways to recognize those who had done well. We held celebrations that had elements of being both special and tied in some way to the business,' Bob explained. When Bob's team expanded into Canada, for example, they celebrated with French vanilla coffee from New York City and French pastries.

MULTI-SENSORY MANAGEMENT

Bob could have spent his time talking at people, rattling off the principles of the organization in rote terms, and micro-managing everything they did. But Bob knew that he needed to take advantage of the brainpower of everyone on his team, from the least to the most skilled person.

He needed extraordinary results from a very diverse group of people – and he needed them fast. This called for extraordinary efforts to unlock people's imaginations and build confidence. It wouldn't take a miracle, but it would take an unconventional approach.

Like juggling.

Juggling?

What in the world does juggling have to do with accounting? (Everything, when it is used as a metaphor for learning how to adapt to change.)

'I knew I had to do something unique with my people if I wanted them to become leaders and change agents,' he explained. 'I wanted them to understand the importance of continuous learning, and that they had unlimited capability. Most people see juggling as difficult. If I could show them that they could master juggling, it would encourage them to try other new challenges.'

Bob knows that people learn better when they are having fun and when they participate actively. He also knows that anyone who has even a small amount of success in juggling will see themselves in a different light. 'In half an hour everyone had learned to juggle,' Bob recalled. 'It was powerful seeing that many people doing something they perceived as difficult or impossible, and being successful at it.'

Bob let everyone keep the training balls he had purchased as a constant reminder of their achievement.

Bob's approach became even more multi-sensory in 1997, when he oversaw the launch for the New Year global accounts payable department. The theme was a spoof of *Star Trek: The Next Generation*, called 'IBM Accounts Payable: The Next Generation'.

The idea was to have employees look into the future and visualize themselves as pioneers in the accounts payable field. To make it memorable, he incorporated all the senses – sight, touch, smell, hearing and taste – and used plenty of imagination.

The 'leaders' of the meeting wore *Star Trek* costumes. Some attendees wore 'Spock ears'. Planets made of Styrofoam balls covered in aluminum foil hung from the ceiling, and there were space ship models on the table. The concept of space with its unlimited galaxies of stars symbolized the unlimited potential for learning and success. The *Star Trek* theme music was played at various points during the programme. Everyone was greeted with a warm handshake when they arrived. They were told to 'smell the success of Accounts Payable in the 21st century' as they enjoyed their coffee, and ate cake decorated with *Star Trek* figures to savour the sweet taste of success.

The programme consisted of skits, which incorporated many cortical skills such as rhythm, space, numbers, words and logic. There was rhythm to the *Star Trek* music, space was everywhere, numbers were important in several of the skits on topics such as electronic fund transfer payments and the Internet, and there was logical thought in the dialogue.

Here is the outline of one of the skits based on a period in 1988 when important accounts payable papers seemed to disappear into a black hole.

A person dressed totally in black with a sign that read 'Black Hole' ran around the room picking up paper and cheques and putting them in her pockets. The mailman walked in and dropped cheques all over the floor. Everything was in disarray.

The skit then showed the future, with efficient employees striving to keep their customers happy. The black hole and mailman characters returned, dressed as before, but wearing signs that said 'Will work for food' – because there was no longer any mail, and the black hole had nothing to do because it could no longer help important documents 'disappear'.

As a constant reminder of what the group was striving for, everyone was given a clock with the emblems 'Starship Enterprise' and 'IBM Accounts

Payable – The Next Generation' on its face to take with them, which can still be seen today on the desks around the office.

'People in my organization recognize that any limits they face are those they've placed on themselves,' said Bob. 'In the early 1990s, we copied a lot of the best practices from other organizations. The trick now is to stay ahead of everyone else. So far, we're managing to do that, and others are now wanting to copy us.'

These technological tools augment the natural tendency of the human brain to learn and seek out new information. They make available to you the skill inventories maintained by others, which will exponentially increase your ability to improve your own skills.

Conclusion

Visions provide the passion, the enthusiasm and the drive to keep on going when the obstacles before you would lead someone without a vision to give up. Visions provide focus and direction for your success-driven brain.

ACTIVITIES

1. **Describe the business vision you have for your company.**

2. **Communicate this business vision to your people. (Think of as many ways as possible.)**

3. **Reinforce this business vision on a daily basis, using as many of the senses as possible.**

4. **Practise writing out what your current situation is regarding your business vision. Be honest, do not make excuses: take responsibility for where you are today.**

5. **Ask each member of your team to describe their current situation (where they presently are) in respect to the business vision.**

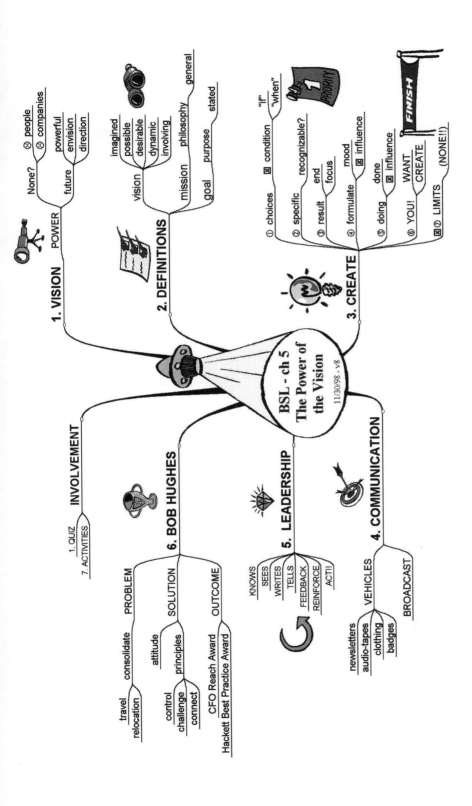

1. VISION

POWER — None?

future — powerful
envision
direction

⊗ people
⊗ companies

2. DEFINITIONS

vision — imagined
possible
desirable
dynamic
involving

mission — philosophy
general

goal — purpose — stated

3. CREATE

① choices — condition — "if"
"when"

② specific — recognizable?

③ result — end
focus

④ formulate — mood
⊠ influence

⑤ doing — done
⊠ influence

⑥ YOU! — WANT
CREATE

⊠⑦ LIMITS — (NONE!!)

INVOLVEMENT
1. QUIZ
7. ACTIVITIES

6. BOB HUGHES

PROBLEM — consolidate — travel
relocation

SOLUTION — attitude
principles — control
challenge
connect

OUTCOME — CFO Reach Award
Hackett Best Practice Award

5. LEADERSHIP

KNOWS
SEES
WRITES
TELLS
FEEDBACK
REINFORCE
ACTI!

4. COMMUNICATION

VEHICLES — newsletters
audio-tapes
clothing
badges

BROADCAST

BSL - ch 5
The Power of the Vision
11/30/98 - v8

6 TEFCAS™: THE SUCCESS FORMULA

Quiz

1. Do you have written corporate goals that you can state?   Yes/No

2. Do you have an internal drive that overcomes any obstacle in reaching your goals?   Yes/No

3. Do you establish 'safe' zones where people can give you honest feedback and not feel threatened by your reaction to receiving it?   Yes/No

4. Do you communicate openly with people regarding their goals?   Yes/No

5. When you give feedback, do you focus on behaviours as opposed to personalities or labels?   Yes/No

6. When you receive feedback, is it unnecessary to check with more than one person for its validity?   Yes/No

7. Are you able to keep taking action even without seeing immediate results?   Yes/No

8. Do you change your goals when receiving unpleasant feedback?   Yes/No

9. Do you learn from mistakes and take corrective action?   Yes/No

10. Do you consider a person's motives when receiving feedback?   Yes/No

SCORING

Score two points for every 'Yes', except question 8 which scores two points for 'No.'

If you scored over 18 points, congratulations! Read on to reinforce your actions, as you already understand the brain's pattern of success. If you scored 18 or less, this chapter will show you how your brain is a success-driven machine.

Overview

In this chapter, you will be introduced to a new way of thinking, known as TEFCAS. TEFCAS is a process for organizing your brain's thinking towards achieving your goals.

The power of TEFCAS

The powerful business tool we are about to introduce to you is not a new computer or any other form of hardware. It is not an innovative piece of software. It won't require that you make radical changes in your office or production line. It won't take months of training.

What it *will* require of you is the willingness to change the way you think, the way you approach problems, the way you work towards your goals.

TEFCAS is an acronym for the steps involved in this new approach to achieving success:

- Trials.
- Events.
- Feedback.
- Check.
- Adjust.
- Success.

In this chapter, we will describe each step, and show you how it can be used to help you reach goals – both your personal goals and your company's.

Your brain is capable of creating limitless thoughts and ideas. Imagine what would happen if you could direct all that creative power towards achieving your chosen goals. That is exactly what happens with TEFCAS.

The end is the beginning

Paradoxically, we are going to start at the end – with the 'S' in TEFCAS.

The 'S' stands for *Success* – the successful outcome, the target or goal. It is what all your efforts are for, what they are designed to accomplish.

Your success, your goal or target, may be a 10 per cent increase in sales for your company, the development of a new widget, or a decrease in employee absenteeism. A personal success or goal might be a promotion, or more time to spend with your family.

We will deal with the other letters in TEFCAS in order, but we start our discussion with the last element because a clear picture of what constitutes success is what makes this powerful tool work.

As we have seen in previous chapters, if you have only a vague idea of your destination when you start out on a journey, you will waste a great deal of time en route. You will take wrong turns, and may end up going in the wrong direction. If you finally arrive, you may not even be aware of it!

Something similar happens when you don't provide your brain with a clear picture of what a successful outcome is, for yourself, your team or your company. The more specific you make the definition, the more effectively your brain will work to achieve that success.

From the Brain Principles (Chapter 3, page 30) you know that the brain links and associates new information to existing knowledge. The brain also likes to 'fill in the blanks' when it receives information that it believes is incomplete. If a goal is vague, each person hearing that goal will generate their own associations about what that goal means. For example, 'being a world class organization' could mean being number one in market share to a sales and marketing person, being first in profitability to a finance person, or having the highest employee morale to a person in human resources. With such a variety of definitions, each person will take actions to move them towards their own understanding of the definition. When the different definitions pull staff in conflicting directions (as could be the case with 'first in market share' versus 'first in profitability'), the results can be disastrous – the brains' rival definitions will lead them to compete against each other, the success mechanism will work against itself, and the organization will suffer.

The commonest single reason for failure in achieving a goal is an unclear definition. Therefore, the first step in applying TEFCAS is to define 'success' as clearly as possible.

In Chapter 3, we said that the brain is a success-driven mechanism (Brain Principle 2) and will work towards whatever has been defined as 'success'. It will work endlessly to bring a successful outcome – *as long as it knows what a successful outcome is*. Before assigning work to their employees, the first thing a Brainsmart Leader does is take the time to articulate carefully and in detail what a successful outcome would be.

Whenever we sat down with an executive, a management team, or a team of employees working on a team project, the very first thing we would ask them to do is to tell us what a successful outcome would be like: 'What are you trying to achieve?' 'What is this thing going to look like when it's finished?' 'What is the end result that we're trying to get to?'

We would find many times that people didn't know what it was they were actually trying to achieve. There would be five people on a team, and they would have five different ideas of what their outcome was supposed to be.

This indicated the organization's misalignment with the goal. And that meant that much extra work was being created. People were working on things that didn't directly relate to the goals they were trying to achieve. And that was because no one ever took the time to clearly define the goals.

Your brain never stops working. All day, it generates thousands of thoughts. It works even when you are asleep, integrating information and creating ideas. If you give it a goal, a target to shoot at, your brain will bend those thoughts, focus them and organize them to find the best way to achieve that goal.

In addition, remember that the brain is not only success-driven, but also truth-seeking (Brain Principle 6). Therefore, the target must be reasonable, one that it is possible to achieve. If you were to select the goal of learning to fly by flapping your arms, for example, your brain would recognize that as impossible, and it would expend little if any effort trying to find a way for you to do it.

The goal should not only be reasonable, it should be something you are enthusiastic about, something you truly want to achieve. If your enthusiasm for the goal is lukewarm, your brain will make only half-hearted efforts to reach it. Therefore, you must examine your commitment towards the goals you want to achieve. Why are they important to you? Will you stop at the first point of resistance, or will you be passionate enough about the goals to devise solutions to any problems that may arise? The answers to these questions will help you understand the level of commitment you have towards your goals.

At this point, you may choose to stop and refine your desired outcome, based on the level of dedication you feel towards it. You are trying to link your goals with your emotional brain, so that your cortical skills blend with your emotional thinking.

Convincing your brain that you truly mean to achieve a goal you set entails using your imagination, – envisioning, feeling, and even tasting the fruits of your efforts. Picture yourself achieving your goal. Feel the handshakes from peers and managers. Hear the words of congratulations. Count the pay rise or rewards that you will receive. Taste the meal celebrating your success.

Blending your cortical skills, your senses and your passion creates the devotion to the outcome that will allow you to consistently overcome obstacles.

BrainSmart!

Use these methods to maximize Success:

- Write down your goals and display them, so that everyone involved can generate thoughts on how to achieve success. Make certain you have the full participation of your team.
- Since the brain generates ideas continuously, 24 hours a day, it is important to have a means to record your thoughts. You could keep a tape recorder or a notepad on your bedside table to capture your ideas.
- Don't pass judgement or set limits to ideas before trying them.
- Abandon the 'we've tried it before and it didn't work' attitude. Try again.
- Try the same idea differently. This time, you may be more successful.

Trials and Try-alls

Once you have provided your brain with a clear goal, one that is achievable and that you are passionately committed to, your brain will automatically go on to the next step of TEFCAS: it will begin trying to achieve that goal through a series of *Trials*.

However, rather than trials, perhaps it would be even more useful to think of the 'T' in TEFCAS as standing for *Try-alls* – for the brain will try everything in order to reach your goal.

You are now unleashing the formidable power of the brain's natural creativity. It knows where you want to go, and it begins generating ideas for how to get there until it finds the path that works. Your thought processes become aligned with your goals. You now have the strongest thinking machine ever created, your brain, working for you to design the path on which you must travel to achieve success.

Since the brain's thought processes are continuous, you are able to generate patterns and design strategies on a 24-hour-a-day basis. Thoughts and ideas may be formed while you are taking a bath, exercising, driving to work, or at 3 a.m. while you are sleeping.

When your brain is on 'automatic pilot', it is uninhibited, free of opinions and judgements. It is at its creative best. And it will continue its generating, creative behaviour as long as you are enthusiastic about achieving the outcome. It has an infinite capacity, and it will persist for as long as you tell it to.

While your brain will continue to work on the best method of reaching your goal automatically, you can help by actively feeding it new information. In the business environment, one way to help facilitate our Try-alls is to find out whether someone else has already achieved our desired outcome. Our brains can then mimic the necessary behaviours or processes (Brain Principle 3). The business term for using the mimic principle is *benchmarking*.

BrainSmart!

Use these techniques in your Try-alls:

- Remember that your brain has an infinite ability to generate ideas. Stay focused on your goal, and give your brain time to generate the Try-alls necessary for success.
- Share your Try-alls with other people who share your definition of success. This will generate new try-alls that you had not previously considered.
- Find suitable models to mimic.
- Assess your persistence level.

A series of events

The Try-all process can be exhilarating. Your brain is generating dozens, perhaps hundreds of ideas intended to help you find your way to your goal. But ideas aren't much use until they are put into action.
The Trials or Try-alls step is the planning stage. The *Events* step is the action stage. We've planned, now it is time to take action. This causes an event.

We use the term 'event' to avoid investing too much importance in a particular occurrence. An event is just one step on the way to success, not the *only* step.

If you start with the idea that the first action you take, the first thing you do to try to achieve your goal is *the* answer, you will be discouraged if it fails, and first steps will often fail to provide you with your defined success. If you accept that an Event is just one step on the journey towards ultimate success, then the fact that it didn't work out (or did) is relatively unimportant.

Too many managers see any Event that doesn't result in progress towards a goal as a failure. They develop that into the idea that they themselves are failures – an attitude that can discourage further efforts. On the other hand, the BrainSmart Leader who recognizes that all Events are part of a process leading to success will accept that unexpected negative results are just as important as – maybe more than – positive ones.

Always remember that the Event is not the goal. Some people remain stuck in the Try-alls stage because they make that mistake. They act as if they

BrainSmart!

Use these techniques for handling Events:

- Events are part of a process, and outcomes should be studied so that you may learn from them.
- As people carry out actions and errors are detected, remember that they are only one Event in the course of the total plan.
- Failure is part of success. Accountability should be assigned to the lessons learned.
- Share what is learned from 'failures' with others.
- Success is also an Event!

have only one chance to succeed, that if one Event fails, then it's all over. With very few exceptions, you will have many more than one opportunity to achieve your success.

Even if the Event does not achieve the desired outcome, you have learned new information that can be used to assist you in reaching your objectives. Events should never be labelled as 'failures', whatever their outcome.

The care and feeding of feedback

To evaluate Events, we need to have some way of providing our brain with information on how well we've done – *Feedback*.

In some ways, Feedback is the most difficult step in TEFCAS, because some of it will be negative. We all have a natural desire to avoid negative feedback. The impulse to 'kill the messenger' when they bring bad news is very common, especially in many executive offices of large organizations.

But in the larger sense, as long as it is honest and focused on the agreed definition of success, there is no such thing as negative Feedback. All Feedback is positive, because it provides us with valuable information. We define 'good' Feedback as any Feedback that helps the person receiving it move closer to achieving their goals.

Good Feedback must be actively sought and encouraged. Far too often, managers and team leaders surround themselves with sycophants who tell them exactly what they want to hear, rather than what they need to hear to be successful. No one wants to tell them that something didn't work as well as was expected, or didn't work at all, so they fudge, equivocate or gloss over any problems.

There is a scene that recurs day after day in many companies. An executive will ask a manager how a new project is going. 'Fine,' the manager may say, 'Everything's going OK.' When the executive leaves, the manager walks down the hall and tells some co-workers, 'This is an utter disaster.' When the manager is asked why they didn't tell the executive the truth, a frequent response is: 'He just doesn't like to hear bad news. And any delay or deviation from plan is perceived as bad news.'

This occurs when executives who request Feedback appear insincere. Perhaps they have been known to heap unfair criticism on others who have told them that a project was going badly. Blaming the messenger for the bad news will only ensure that bad news never reaches the boss until it is *really* bad news – and too late.

In addition to making it clear that you want honest Feedback, you must make it equally clear that you want the feedback to be as specific and detailed as possible. Feedback should also be directly related to the goal.

Take the example of an executive who wants their junior managers to work more closely as a team. If they ask for Feedback on how well the team concept is working, they need detailed examples of exactly what is happening, and how it relates to the goal.

Good Feedback from an observer might be the following:

> You say your goal is to have your managers sit down as a team to develop recommendations for this new project. But some of your managers won't even talk to each other. Others are making individual decisions that are costing time and money. And some managers are arguing and attacking each other publicly.

That would be excellent Feedback, because it is specific enough for the executive to see where they are going to have to make some changes. The Feedback is also honest, and directly relates to the goal of bonding the managers into a team.

Feedback is not a one-way process. You must be prepared to give it as well as receive it. The same rules apply whether giving or receiving Feedback: it must be honest, specific and related to the goal.

When offering Feedback to someone else, you must know what their goal is. If you wish to provide Feedback to a subordinate, you must know what that subordinate's goal is, what they consider a successful outcome.

If the subordinate is a foreman who has told you he wants to be the best foreman in the city, your Feedback should take that into account. For example, you might say something like the following:

> Harry, your procrastination in getting your paperwork done on time hurts both the company and yourself. Erratic delivery of supplies means we sometimes have to shut jobs down. And that certainly doesn't contribute to your goal of being the best foreman in the city.

When you give Feedback that is tied to the goals of the person receiving it, you also avoid personal and emotional confrontation. The issue becomes the actions that need to be taken or adjustments that need to be made, rather than issues of personality or character. You aren't telling anyone that they are a bad person, only that they need to do certain things differently (adjust their Try-alls) to achieve their goal.

Without Feedback, we can only assume that the path we are following will lead to our goals. In this case, we are filling in the blanks generated in our brain with nothing more than suppositions and hypotheses. Truth-seeking Feedback is the lifeline to Success. Useful Feedback provides a measurement of the effectiveness of the actions we've chosen to take in order to achieve our goals. It also provides us with the data to plan towards future Adjustments and Try-alls that will be necessary in order for us to reach Success.

Check the feedback

After you have received Feedback, you need to *Check* whether it is valid and accurate.

If the Feedback given is inaccurate or incomplete, then if you act on it, your journey to success may be jeopardized. Therefore, any Feedback you receive should be assessed to determine if it has merit. The best way to check Feedback is to compare it to Feedback from known reliable sources.

BrainSmart!

Use the following techniques in receiving Feedback:

- Always check Feedback for accuracy and alignment with your goals.
- Invite and encourage Feedback. Don't assume that it will automatically be given.
- Don't react defensively to Feedback if you did not like it.

Use the following techniques when giving Feedback:

- Express your Feedback in a way that encourages the receiver to hear what you are saying.
- Keep faith and confidence in the value of your Feedback. Always remember to incorporate good news when sharing Feedback that may be perceived as negative.
- Always make sure that the recipient of Feedback is in an open state of mind to receive Feedback.
- Link all Feedback to the goals.
- Give Feedback to yourself as well.

If a foreman who was told that filing his paperwork late was a problem wanted to check that Feedback, he could ask several other people (peers, subordinates, other executives within the organization) if they agreed with that assessment. However, if you do decide to ask a subordinate, if the Feedback is to have integrity, they must not feel threatened and thus obligated to give you the answer they think you want.

In addition, once you have checked the Feedback you have received, you must accept it. If you perceive it to be inaccurate, then it may have a negative impact on your thought processes. Remember that the brain is truth-seeking (Brain Principle 6), and if it doubts the integrity of the input, it will discard it accordingly. The blind acceptance of Feedback without checking to confirm that it is factual, relevant and effective, could introduce negative inputs which could redirect your action plan away from your goals.

Accurate Feedback is invaluable, and can lead us to reach our goals, as we exercise our prerogative to act on shared information and knowledge. All Feedback received should be assessed to establish whether it is warranted and justified. Once Feedback has been checked, it can then be used to change and Adjust action plans we've devised, to bring us one more step closer to achieving Success.

BrainSmart!

Use these techniques in Checking:

- Occasionally Check your goal, to ensure that it is still relevant.
- Check Feedback to verify that it is specific and measurable.
- Check whether an Event took you closer to or further from your goal.
- Check the action you need to take next.

Making adjustments

The 'A' in TEFCAS stands for *Adjust*. It is the final step on the way to 'S', the Successful outcome of your goal.

Adjusting is the moment of truth. After defining your goals, considering Try-alls, performing Events, receiving Feedback and Checking, you must decide whether to Adjust your actions – and if so, how. In this stage, once you have accepted the Feedback as accurate, you will begin to Adjust your actions so that you achieve your goal.

When you reach this point, you may be reluctant to Adjust your Try-alls. You may resist the idea of doing things differently. Instead of modifying your actions, you may instead rationalize: 'Well, I didn't want to be director

BrainSmart!

Use the following techniques to Adjust:

- Your brain will Adjust for the next Try-all. *You* determine what will be Adjusted.
- As long as you are committed to achieving your goal, don't give up at the 'moment of truth' stage.
- Allow your brain to find alternative solutions.
- Sometimes just a minor Adjustment will lead you to success. Don't assume that an Adjustment to your Try-alls must involve radical change.
- Consider looking for different perspectives from different people when creating new action plans. You may use benchmarking or other sources of ideas.

of my department by next April. Being manager is just fine with me.'
When this happens, you are not Adjusting your Try-alls, but instead are
adjusting your definition of Success – you are Adjusting your goal, rather
than your action. Sometimes this may be appropriate, but if you retain
your goal and keep it in mind, your brain will create new Try-alls to generate
different Events until it achieves Success. You will begin to Adjust the
actions that must be taken to achieve your goal.

TEFCAS summary

The steps of TEFCAS are:

1. **Define success,** as the brain is success-driven and needs a clear goal
   towards which it can work.
2. **Try-all** the suggestions your brain creates in its attempt to map out the
   course of action you must take to succeed.
3. **An Event** will occur as a result of the Try-all you implemented.
4. **Receive Feedback,** from yourself and others.
5. **Check** before you accept the information, as the brain is truth-seeking,
   and needs accurate data to adjust.
6. **Adjust** according to the Feedback you gathered.
7. Repeat the TEFCAS process as necessary.
8. **Attain Success,** as you defined it.
9. Celebrate!

Test this model by applying it to a situation where you are currently not
as successful as you would like to be, and you will begin to see how you
can use TEFCAS to reach your goals. Figure 6.1 summarizes the model
in graphic form.

Leadership profile: Candace Jones

The Holiday Inn Arena in Binghamton, New York, wasn't the worst
Holiday Inn in the region, but it was near the bottom in customer
satisfaction.

At the helm was general manager Candace Jones, a perfectionist with a
sincere desire to make the hotel a winner – a desire that seemed to be
constantly thwarted by intangible factors she couldn't quite identify. All
she knew for sure was that poor morale, lack of initiative and a pervasive
attitude that anything that went wrong was somebody else's problem was
translating into unhappy guests.

The Brain's Success Mechanism Follows a Consistent Model

T	E	F	C	A	S
Try-all	Event	Feedback	Check	Adjust	Success
Attempt to make progress towards your goal.	Something happens, moving you closer to or further from your goal.	Receive Feedback related to the event, from yourself and others.	Check the Feedback for accuracy and relevance.	Act upon the Feedback. Adjust your next Try-all or your Success definition.	Succeed! Keep following the first five steps and you will reach your goal!

Iterations

Repetition
Reduces
Resistance

Figure 6.1 The TEFCAS model

One of those unhappy guests was Tony Dottino, who stayed at the Holiday Inn Arena in August 1996. There had been serious problems with the hotel's air conditioning system, and after three room changes, Tony's temper was as hot as the rest of him.

Candace directed that a letter be written to Tony, offering free accommodation on his next visit. 'Tell him if he tries us again and we still can't get it right, then we don't deserve his business', Candace said.

When Tony received the letter, he was impressed, and noted the fact that Candace seemed committed to making her customers happy. So the next time he was in Binghamton, Tony stayed at the Arena, this time meeting Candace.

When Candace learned about Tony's line of work, she was intrigued. Maybe he could shed some light on her problems. As the two strolled around the hotel golf course, Tony asked Candace, 'What is your definition of success?' She told him that she wanted to take the hotel 'further'. He pressed her to elaborate, and realized that part of her frustration was the result of her failure to communicate a clear picture of success to her staff, because she didn't have a clear enough idea in her own head of what she wanted.

Tony finally wrested from her what she wanted to do: treat every guest like a VIP, and create an atmosphere as much like home as possible for them. However, Tony noticed that there was some negativity on her part. It was agreed to start a Mental Literacy training programme.

In their first session, Tony asked hotel staff to Mind Map their frustrations. What they revealed was astonishing. 'Many times in meetings I had asked, "How am I doing?", but they were never comfortable giving me the unpleasant truth', said Candace. 'At the session with Tony, however, they did speak their minds. It wasn't easy listening, but it was a positive step, because it forced me to come to grips with some things I needed to improve upon.'

Candace learned that she treated her staff like incompetent children. For example, one day she had led all the managers around the hotel looking for problem areas. There were cobwebs on the ceiling. The brass in the bar wasn't polished. A storage closet was a mess. 'I'm totally disappointed in you', she lectured them. 'You are supposed to be professionals. Why do I have to baby-sit you?'

Humiliated, embarrassed and demoralized, no one was brave enough, until the session with Tony, to answer her question. Without realizing it, Candace had sapped everyone's desire to take initiative, because whenever anyone did something on their own, she'd take it over, criticize the way they had done it, or instruct them to do it some other way.

'I was frustrated, and thought they weren't supporting me by taking the ball and running with it, but how could they run with it when any time they tried, I'd intercept it?' she said. 'My approach made them feel, "Why bother if she's going to do it herself anyway?" '

The first step in tackling this problem of control – and it was a big step for Candace – was to let go, delegate, and accept the fact that there was more than one right way to handle a situation. When Tony asked employees to Mind Map what they thought Candace's goals were, none of them matched the Mind Map Candace drew. It was quickly obvious why she hadn't been getting the results she had sought – everyone had a different idea of what she wanted.

'I'd tell people I wanted to take the hotel further, and they'd nod, but no one ever asked me, "What are you talking about?" ' Candace remembered. 'I just assumed they knew, and their misunderstanding made it even more frustrating. When they did something other than what I wanted, I assumed they weren't in my boat, rowing with me.'

Once that problem was acknowledged, they worked together to create a group Mind Map, to come to a consensus about what specific steps needed to be taken for success. It was agreed that customer satisfaction was the most important result, so their central image was a big smile.

'To me, friendliness and a positive attitude were *major* points,' Candace related, 'and I knew they were contagious – a smile from me would transfer to my staff, and down to the customer. I realized that any time I passed on a bad mood to my managers, they were likely to pass that on to staff, and then on to guests. I realized that my behaviour was duplicated all the way through the organization. Looking back at the smile on the Mind Map, I was forced to acknowledge that the buck truly stopped with me.'

The exercise also helped Candace discover who would never be 'in her boat'. 'This was the first time I had ever seen my teams clearly,' she said. 'Two people ended up leaving our employ, and it was much easier to deal with their decision to leave after seeing their Mind Maps.' Finding replacements for those two people was easier because she had a clearer idea of who would be an appropriate team member.

With all these changes, the hotel is running smoothly, and morale is considerably improved. 'My goal is to continue development of staff and the management team by allowing them to feel a part of the decision-making process,' Candace said.

When the hotel decided recently to change the theme of its restaurant, Candace told staff to form a committee and come up with ideas. 'Before, I would have come up with the idea and said to them, "Now go do it," ' she explained. Employees – from housekeeping staff to managers – now have permission to make and act upon decisions affecting guests without checking first with their superiors. 'They feel more ownership that way,' explained Candace. 'They aren't just taking orders, but are part of the process. We have empowered the staff to make decisions, and they make good ones because they know I'll back them up.'

And the best part? The guests are happier, because they get immediate results.

While Candace was busy improving her management style and employee morale, she was dealing with other challenges as well. At the time she took over, Binghamton was a city in decline, and the Holiday Inn Arena was right in the middle of that city. People were shopping in the suburbs, and businesses were flocking to areas near main traffic arteries.

The situation was bleak, the looming future even bleaker. There was doubt whether the hotel would survive. Two large companies had recently moved out, taking 3 000 people with them. Occupancy was at an all-time low.

Candace identified the main problems, and analysed them. She then began looking for ways to overcome them. Try-alls from the TEFCAS model would ultimately save the hotel. Instead of sitting around wringing her hands and reacting, she decided to take action.

She identified the following negative factors:

- The hotel's mainstay in the past, corporate bookings, had reduced drastically because there were few businesses left in the vicinity.
- The hotel didn't have much to offer in the way of entertainment.
- People preferred more expensive hotels in better locations.
- The rooms were small.

Candace conceived ways to turn these negatives into positives.

Since corporate bookings were down, they needed to attract different customers. She decided to market her hotel as an affordable destination for golfers. She forged deals with local golf courses, went to travel trade shows, and developed brochures. By the second year, 27 per cent of the increased occupancy was due to golfers.

With so many companies going through budget squeezes, she advertised the hotel as an inexpensive venue for conventions, and enticed them further by offering to stage special theme parties, such as a Mardi Gras night. The hotel also offered the services of a meeting planner at no extra charge, making it so easy to hold a convention there that it became a favourite location.

During those dismal weeks from January through March when occupancy had usually been so low employees had to be laid off, the hotel offered skiing and horseback riding packages at nearby resorts, and courted tour bus operators. 'We began attracting nine or ten busloads every weekend, with 400–500 people. This resulted in a very significant increase in revenue,' Candace says.

Instead of being apologetic about the size of the rooms, they marketed them as 'cosy', and made sure that everyone was friendly, welcoming and helpful at all times. 'We know we aren't the Ritz Carlton, so we made it our goal for every customer to leave saying it was the best stay they'd ever had. We wanted them to leave with a smile on their face – to feel like they had found a little piece of home here.'

Finally, Candace joined the tourism committee of the local chamber of commerce, whose goal is to 'change the identity of Binghamton'. 'I believe this city can come back and flourish, and that the success we've had here at the hotel will ripple throughout the city,' says Candace.

Since Candace joined the Holiday Inn Arena team, overall revenue has increased by 35 per cent, occupancy has increased by 13 per cent, and the hotel's customer satisfaction rating has leapt from twenty-fifth in the company to eighth.

It wasn't easy, but Candace did it. She transformed the hotel's fortunes, and those of many others, and made the Holiday Inn Arena a very fine place to work and to stay.

Conclusion

TEFCAS's applications are limitless, and it can be used to define your next course of action. TEFCAS is a powerful tool that allows you to be in control of the problems you face every day in order to ensure your success. The authors use it constantly, and are convinced of its power and influence.

ACTIVITIES

1. Write definitions of both your business and personal desired outcomes.

2. Create a Mind Map of all the ideas you generate to make progress towards your goal.

3. Develop a support group of three people with whom you can share and develop your goals.

4. Practise giving Feedback to a business associate where you can provide information about specific behaviours you have observed which cause him or her to miss their goal. Provide suggestions on how you think he or she could do better. (Note: always ask the person first if he or she would like Feedback.)

5. Next time someone gives you Feedback, verify the Feedback with at least two other sources. List both the consistencies and the inconsistencies.

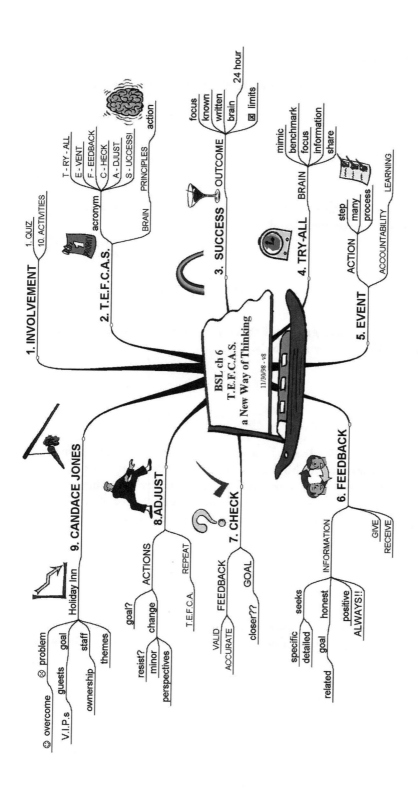

7 THE BRAINSMART LEADER

Quiz

1. Do you consider your people to be the primary asset of your company?   Yes/No

2. Do you believe that without trust and confidence a successful business relationship is possible?   Yes/No

3. Are you constantly assessing the skills needed by your company to remain competitive?   Yes/No

4. Do you know the skill gap that exists between your current employees' skills and your future needs?   Yes/No

5. Have you and your employees designed an education plan for developing their skill level?   Yes/No

6. Do you speak highly of your employees to other people?   Yes/No

7. Do you spend more than a third of your day putting out fires?   Yes/No

8. Can you take a holiday and be confident that your operation will run smoothly?   Yes/No

9. Do you believe that your behaviours are both watched and copied by your employees?   Yes/No

10. Do you believe that the responsibility for coaching your employees lies with the human resources department?   Yes/No

SCORING

Score two points for each 'yes', except for questions 2, 7 and 10 which score two points for 'No'. If you scored 18 or more you have excellent management leadership skills. This chapter will help you fine-tune them. If you scored less than 18, this chapter will show you how to develop these important communication skills with your workforce.

Overview

This chapter illustrates by means of a case study how leaders can apply the Brain Principles covered in Chapter 3 to build trust and confidence within their teams. Communication is vital for a BrainSmart Leader, so we explore this in detail.

BrainSmart Leadership

Few would dispute that the most significant asset of any company is its workforce. Since this belief has become so widespread, why do so many companies still continue to squander the intelligence of their employees? How many annual reports have you read where the company refers to its employees as its most valuable asset, only to announce a downsizing resulting in thousands of redundancies soon after?

How can you realize the potential of your staff? By harnessing their power and tapping into their natural creativity and Intellectual Capital, as described in this book.

Like any valuable asset, the intelligence of your workforce must be maintained and nurtured by providing an atmosphere that is both challenging and stimulating. As we mentioned in Chapter 3, the brain needs to continually learn new information in order to remain vibrant and creative (Brain Principle 5). One way to accomplish this is to encourage your employees to continue their education, whether internally through company-sponsored training programmes or externally through university courses. Since the main objective of education is to exercise their brains, studying topics with which they are unfamiliar will be most beneficial.

To secure the greatest return from your human assets, you must realize that *everyone* is creative. Your ability to tap into the excitement, enthusiasm and energy of your staff will ultimately determine the long-term performance of your company. Managed properly, the combined intelligence of your employees will lead to success; managed poorly, it will lead to disaster.

Consider the results a group of people can generate when they are committed to a leader with a clearly defined goal. To make the best use of this power, the leader must encourage everyone in the group to ask:

'What is the best way to relate to people?' and 'How does my thinking mechanism work?'

Great managers are great coaches

The next time you watch a sporting event featuring a team that consistently wins, observe the coach. Effective coaches play several roles that are essential to their teams' performance. They need to be visionaries, with a clear picture of what their programmes and teams must accomplish. They must be excellent communicators, defining this vision clearly for their players so that they also believe in it. They must motivate and inspire their players. They must be teachers, providing their players with the technical instruction necessary to make the most of their ability, and they must evaluate talent, offering feedback on performance so that their players know how well or poorly they are performing. Although coaches don't throw, kick or hit the ball during matches, their ability to fulfil these roles determines whether their teams will win or lose.

BrainSmart Leaders are coaches. They have to encourage their staff to stretch their limits to perform in ways they never thought possible. They must communicate their executive team's vision to their managers and staff, building them into a team which can work cohesively to translate the vision into reality.

BrainSmart Leaders do this by understanding the workings of the brain, applying the seven Brain Principles and TEFCAS to the structure of their work and their teams to achieve maximum impact.

CASE STUDY

An Unsuccessful Manager

Joe Friday is a successful staff accountant with XYZ Corporation. Joe's department is responsible for reporting the business results of the domestic operations for his company's manufacturing and service organizations. One day, Joe received a call from Personnel, saying that as a result of organizational changes, they were sending him a new manager, Jane Doe, and moving the present manager, Mike Merryfield, to the Export Accounts division. Although Jane had managed other groups within the business results reporting function, she had no firsthand experience with Joe's department.

To make her transition to the new department as smooth as possible, Mike spent a few days showing her the ropes. He introduced her to the staff who handled the main activities of the department, and explained the processes that existed within it. Because of Mike Merryfield's hiring pattern and emphasis on training, the staff combined many areas of expertise, with a balance of technical and practical knowledge.

Once Jane began to play a more active role, the staff quickly noticed the conflict between her leadership style and that of Mike. Before the first month had passed under her management, Jane held a departmental meeting where she laid down many new rules without explaining why they were necessary. Although all her staff worked on a fixed-salary basis, Jane demanded that they notify her whenever they took a break for lunch or any other reason. The new rules and oppressive supervision started to create mistrust.

Jane expressed concern that her staff were unable to analyse the output of their work properly. Her solution was to require them to provide her with finalized data earlier than the normal set schedule. This request alarmed the staff, because they had already reduced their cycle time considerably, and further reduction would require a large-scale redirection of their

efforts. Furthermore, it did not match the department's goals for the year.

Staff trust and confidence continued to decline over time, and tension continued to build within the department. In later departmental meetings, Jane publicly reprimanded staff members for making mistakes, even when they resulted from trying to formulate new solutions to improve the service for important customers. She demanded to be notified of all new projects, regardless of scope, for pre-approval. During one of the meetings, Jane declared that all staff members were required to work the following weekend, even though several team members had already made travel plans with their families.

The group's frustration continued to increase when they discussed the meetings among themselves. Every team member noted the difference in the morale and focus of the department. Lack of trust and confidence in management grew as the department began work on a new special project.

Jane seemed to welcome ideas and input at project meetings, but she never followed anything through. If a minor change was proposed from the original plan for the project, Jane resisted it.

This inconsistency led to a lack of a clear direction towards any goals. Jane behaved as if she felt she could not rely on anyone in her department, and must carry its workload alone.

The staff soon found that Jane became easily frustrated by any deviation from her expectations of their performance. Her motto became: 'I want *everything* to work *perfectly*, *all* the time.' Because of the changes rippling throughout the organization, this goal was seen as impossible. The team had traditionally worked to provide low error rates combined with creative solutions for new issues as they arose. As it became evident that *any* mistakes would be punished by humiliation, less innovative and creative ideas were generated by the department, since creative ideas represented such a high risk, and everyone became preoccupied with minimizing the chance of being blamed. The unfortunate consequence of this mindset was that it united the Intellectual Capital ability of the department – but against its leader! The survival instincts of the employees meant that each member developed a defensive attitude regarding any issue linked to Jane.

A silent civil war ensued, with

both sides interested only in winning small battles. The frustrated, demotivated 'subjects' withdrew from their despotic, intolerant 'ruler'. Communication between the staff and Jane became selective, and problems were hidden.

Departmental meetings became silent, and creativity evaporated. There was no leadership to provide the guidance necessary to align the department towards its goals. All of this led to an unexcited, unenthusiastic

workforce, resulting in customer dissatisfaction. With the erosion of the trust and confidence in their leader, the team was unable to begin a communication process to address its concerns.

Trust and confidence: The brain is truth-seeking (Brain Principle 6)

Surveys have shown that people consider trust and confidence the most important factor determining how they communicate and interact with each other. When building relationships, trust is bestowed upon others cautiously, like a precious gift. It takes time to develop, and once betrayed, never fully returns. When it is present, it opens doors, breaks down walls, and unleashes creativity. Trust increases our willingness to listen to new ideas and to take risks. Lack of trust causes us to retreat to safe territory, and inhibits our ability to think freely and creatively. Trust must be earned, and once won, should be nurtured carefully.

Since Brain Principle 6 tells us that the brain is a truth-seeking device that acts on what it believes to be true, the results of these surveys should be no surprise. A BrainSmart Leader should recognize the power of this principle to ensure that their staff focuses and takes action towards reaching a common goal. How much easier it would have been for Jane if she had shared her goals with her department, and created a group consensus. She would not have felt she had to do everything on her own, and more importantly, she would have tapped into the natural thinking processes of her experienced staff.

With the advent of re-engineering programmes, the job security of many employees has been threatened. As changes are introduced into the organization, sharing information plays an even more critical role.

The brain seeks knowledge and information so that it can make connections and associations about a topic (Brain Principle 5). When it is given inaccurate or incomplete information, or no information at all, it will work to fill in the blanks (Brain Principle 4). The synergy principle (Brain

Principle 1) comes into play, and the brain generates possible scenarios, fuelling the rumour mill.

If a management team wants to restrict the influence of the rumour mill, it needs to communicate information to its staff that fills in the blanks in a way this is credible. The people who hear this information will then be able to use the synergy principle to take appropriate action. This leads to a natural process which generates ideas that can provide innovative solutions to customer needs and business problems, and build enthusiasm among the group.

Since the success of any organizational change effort is largely determined by the creativity of team members and their willingness to take risks, it is vital to earn and maintain their trust. An effective way to do this is to share information with them so they can generate solutions that are focused on the correct goals. Senior management must always try to create an environment where trust and confidence can be built and nourished, and recognize that the words they use and actions they take will be mimicked by their staff (Brain Principle 3).

Companies where trust is low or non-existent tend to have high staff turnover. Although employees are generally encouraged to continue their education in order to keep their skill sets current, a company with a low-trust environment that pays for its staff's education will not benefit from its investment, since employees will take the benefit of this training to another company with whom they are more comfortable. Thus, low-trust companies find themselves in a double bind: if they invest in training their employees, they will not reap the full benefit because the additional skills make it easier for unhappy employees to find better jobs with a competitor, whereas if they restrict the marketability of their employees by limiting training, their workforce's skills will become outdated, and eventually obsolete. In either case, their Intellectual Capital will be drained until it cannot sustain performance.

The importance of communicating any changes in your company's missions and goals to your employees must not be underestimated, as they are more likely to trust you. Employees with diverse and up-to-date skills can recover from adversity and transform themselves much more easily and quickly. Contemplate the same situation in a company with outdated skill sets where no trust exists. The workforce will become defensive, risk-averse and sceptical, with everyone watching their backs. Some disgruntled employees may even secretly delight in the failure of the company, as just deserts for past sins. An unhappy employee may even regard the collapse of the company as success!

Successful managers do not just build trust within their own organization. To remain successful, a company must have strong relationships with its customers, built upon trust and reliability. For example, if you promise a customer 100 per cent of their requirements, you will disappoint them if you deliver only 80 per cent. On the other hand, you could notify your customer that the best you can deliver is 80 per cent of what is requested, but ensure you do so. In the former case, there will be anger, mistrust and you may lose future business. In the latter, there are no broken promises, the relationship with your customer is not jeopardized, and the customer's trust in you will be maintained or strengthened. The customer received what was promised, even though it was less than what they wanted, so they could make contingency plans.

Jane Doe from XYZ imposed new rules on her staff without taking the time to explain the reasons for them. This created mental blanks in the minds of her staff that were filled with scenarios of mistrust and hostility. An ineffective manager who tries to implement new rules unilaterally will meet resistance and cynicism. New rules that are not explained to staff are likely to be bent or broken. In the case of Jane Doe, departmental meetings were negative experiences for everyone, adding to the mistrust. The brains of the departmental staff used the negative inputs from these meetings to create new links and associations, which were also negative. Their brains also invoked the mimic principle (Brain Principle 3) to model the excessive criticism and lack of trust demonstrated by Jane. The combination of all these factors eventually turned the department against its leader.

BrainSmart Leaders can introduce new rules easily because they develop trusting relationships with their employees. They first gain their trust by confiding the reason behind the new rules and justifying their actions. They reinforce this trust by inviting feedback from their employees. They do not become defensive when faced with criticism, and are willing to change or eliminate rules that prove to be unsound after hearing their employees' views. They may request the assistance of their more experienced staff to make the transition easier.

When Jane was setting new goals, she achieved neither consensus nor alignment, and she failed to give credit to the group for work they had already done. When establishing new goals, it is always important to explain to your staff the need for them, especially if they need to stretch themselves to achieve it. If your staff feel the new goal is impossible and feel no ownership in setting it, they will not draw on the persistence principle (Brain Principle 7). Their brains will not generate ways to achieve the goal, but reasons why it cannot be achieved.

The public humiliation and reprimands for failure further compounded the resistance Jane's staff displayed towards the new goals. These attacks triggered her employees' defence mechanisms. Had Jane approached failures by saying, 'How interesting, what can we learn from this?', she would have unleashed creative, positive thinking.

Leonardo DaVinci believed that everything connects to everything else, and a manager must realize that a person's brain does not shut off work issues while at home, nor ignore home issues while at work. Several of her employees had already made travel plans with their families that could be cancelled only with great difficulty. Forcing an employee to choose between work and family divides the attention of the brain, rather than letting its thoughts flow naturally. As a result, the employees who gave up time with their families to work mandatory weekends spent much more time at work thinking about their families than they would have otherwise: 'I really miss my family. I am angry that Jane's worries about our schedule have taken priority over my personal time. Jane is more concerned about her own success then with keeping my morale high.' This further increased the tension between Jane and her staff, and fostered an 'us against them' mentality.

Trust and confidence provide the climate that allows open, two-way communication to take place. This communication of information and knowledge allows our brain to make appropriate corrections towards the achievement of its goals, and provides the basis for building long-lasting relationships.

Trust and confidence are key factors in determining a company's ability to implement change and make full use of its existing Intellectual Capital. The synergy of creative thought processes is more effective when it operates in a comfortable and trusting environment. To be successful, each manager must produce a stable environment that allows any potentially risky situation to be evaluated with mutual respect. If the uncharted pathways of our brains are thought to be littered with mines, no one will take the risk of attempting to travel on them by coming up with new ideas.

BrainSmart!

Here are some observations on trust and confidence:

- Use as many of your five senses and the ten cortical skills as possible to convey the exact meaning of your thoughts.
- Remember that the brain is truth-seeking, and acts on what it believes to be true
- Respect the trust others have in you.
- Remember the importance of feedback.
- Be caringly honest with others.
- Be aware of the environment around you.
- Remember that it takes time to earn trust.

From the brain's point of view, trust and confidence translate into truth and belief, so BrainSmart Leaders should concentrate on building trust and confidence with their employees.

Communication

The brain learns best through association, by linking new information to existing information in a synergistic fashion. Your life experiences define the connections your brain makes between two pieces of information in a fashion that is unique to you.

To maximize the effectiveness of your communication, learn to communicate using skills from both sides of your brain. In addition to communicating numbers, facts and statistics (left cortex), you must also use images, colours and rhythm (right cortex), but remember that because no two brains are identical, the mental picture you have of what you are communicating may differ from that formed by your listener. We are only familiar with our own associations, so we cannot assume that the same reactions and responses will exist in others. Consider, for example, what temperature would be considered a 'warm day' by a resident of New York compared to someone from Florida. Contemplate the confusion among the different functions of an organization when the executive team promises 'dramatic' work and performance improvements because of a new re-engineering programme. Imagine the variety of responses when company leaders are asked to quantify what they mean by 'dramatic' or 'significant', and the problems that could result.

Very often when people are introduced to others, they are labelled by the person introducing them. If we know the person making the introduction, these labels are often accepted as 'truth' by our brain before it makes its own determination of the validity of the label. You have probably seen examples of this when listening to two different people describe the same object or person. Have you ever wondered how two people can view the same object and have totally different perspectives?

When Joe explained the processes, it is likely that he left blanks in Jane's mind. A manager often lacks sufficient details to explain problems or issues to someone else properly, so detailed explanations of unfamiliar processes are best left to the person who does the work. A BrainSmart Leader who joins a new organization can use this knowledge to help understand the organization by determining whether the person doing the explaining is filling in blanks or creating them – an excellent way to evaluate how well a person knows their job.

Unfamiliarity with every detail of a new department can exacerbate the normal feeling of being overwhelmed that a new manager experiences when taking on a new position. The manager's thoughts in this instance can be best described as: 'I hope someone here knows what's going on until I figure out how to survive.'

While it is relatively easy to transfer information by speaking, it is very difficult to truly *communicate* while speaking, since the same word can trigger different associations in different people. Communicating effectively with someone requires that you communicate 'brain to brain'. A combination of trust and your knowledge of the skills inventory of your listener is helpful here: you can use these to communicate in a fashion that links your thoughts to their cortical skills through their five senses. With this is mind, you should begin a topic of conversation by asking some key questions to establish a base of information and knowledge.

Because of Mike's training, the staff had areas of expertise, including a balance of technical and practical knowledge. Jane could have assessed the skills of her department in terms of the ten cortical skills of the brain to assess the strengths and weaknesses of the group as a whole. For example, sitting with each person to learn about their job, she could map their dominant cortical skills onto the matrix shown in Chapter 4. By doing so, Jane could draw up an inventory of the skills of the department and see if there were any cortical skills missing, such as 'big picture' thinking, imagination, logic, or lack of details and technical knowledge.

Words are powerful communication tools, and they evoke a multiplicity of associations that cause us to interpret them individually, as uniquely as our experiences. To show the power of the associations of words, draw a circle with the word 'money' at the centre, and draw ten lines radiating from the circle. Think of ten words that you associate with money, and write one word on each line. Keep your responses to yourself. Then ask four other people you know to perform the same exercise on their own. When you have all completed the exercise, compare your ten words with the others, looking for complete matches. With a group of four people, it is quite common to find no matches at all. At best, you may find one or two word matches between two people.

Jane alienated her entire department after the first meeting by communicating requirements that implied that the department was not trustworthy. The associations to this message – whether conscious or unconscious – evoked resentment and defensiveness among her staff. Had Jane communicated her concerns to the department, recognizing the associations that her team would make, they could have worked together to develop a solution which addressed her concerns, but in a much friendlier atmosphere. For example, Jane could have asked to be kept updated on new projects, not simply for pre-approval (which implied that she was the only person who could be trusted to decide whether or not a project should be undertaken), but because she needed the knowledge to manage the workload of her department more effectively (which would have implied concern about keeping the workload manageable and equitable). Both requests would have asked for the same information, but the latter would have resulted in a much less hostile environment.

All these opportunities could have provided the staff with an excellent role model and coach to mimic. Imagine the influence she could generate by being the model for building trust and confidence, leading to open communication. Through this model, the staff would have a basis to share their concerns with her. This opening could provide them with the possibility to persist and not feel so helpless when generating ideas to reach their organizational goals. Finally, in trying to gain the knowledge and information necessary to make her comfortable as quickly as possible, the group could have drawn up Mind Maps to assist the communication process.

When communicating with someone, whenever possible, create a picture or image in the mind of the listener, using vivid words that describe the

BrainSmart!

Here are some other suggestions for improving communication:

- In building trust and confidence and setting the course of communication in a relationship, you may begin by asking a person what they view as the important values and standards they use to measure their progress over time.
- Lead a group. Take responsibility for leading a team (for example, in a hobby or a skill that you have mastered).
- Share knowledge with the people in your work environment or home life.
- Focus more on communication skills that appeal to all five senses and to all ten cortical skills.
- Check your communication – ask for feedback on the meanings and associations you created while communicating.

scene. If the image is clear and trust exists between speaker and listener, the concept is quickly understood and immediately accepted.

A trust-filled environment with open communication channels plus effective communication leads to infinite creativity. Imagine a workplace where innovation and breakthroughs happen regularly. Think of a company where people are excited and motivated about their jobs, where they actually look forward to coming to work each day. At this company, productivity is world-class because open and honest communication channels across all functions and levels of management allow problems to be quickly identified, communicated and resolved. Risk-taking is considered an important part of the creative process, and failures are viewed as providing a unique opportunity to learn. Customers rave about the quality of service provided, and feel their input is valued and respected.

Now consider the alternative. Picture a workplace where innovation is scarce, and risk-taking is openly discouraged. 'If it was a good idea, somebody would have already thought of it' is the company motto. Information is viewed as a jealously guarded asset, and is shared on a 'need-to-know' basis only. Communication serves merely to transfer limited information back and forth, but the information is fragmented, and frequently taken out of context. The workforce is cynical about attempts to improve working conditions or customer service, and staff turnover is high. Productivity is low, and continues to deteriorate as each person protects themself, and avoiding blame for mistakes wastes energy. Competition among departments is fierce, and the failure of other departments is viewed as an opportunity for your own department to look better in the eyes of senior management.

Which company would you rather work for? Which company do you think will outperform the other? Which company do you think will eventually be struggling just to survive?

The assets of a company reside in the skills of each individual. It is the ability of a BrainSmart Leader to nurture these skills which leads a company to long-term success. In your interaction with others, you have the opportunity to establish a model for others to follow. So what will it be? Will your communication be honest and helpful, or disingenuous and misleading? Will your work environment be exciting and encourage innovation, or boring and encourage finger-pointing? Will your communication be interesting and informative, or dull and useless? You decide.

Leadership profile: Sandy Hahn, IBM

Sandy Hahn manages the Change Integration department at IBM. She knows how to motivate her staff. As a result, her team of six employees saved the company $1 million a year between 1996 and 1998.

In early 1996, Sandy was asked to simplify the system used by IBM employees working overseas (known as 'international assignees') who have to file relocation expenses. The previous system involved assignees laboriously filling out complicated paperwork by hand. That paperwork was then transferred to the International Assignment Accounting organization for processing. This processing required someone to key the information into a computer.

The process was confusing for the assignee, there were many opportunities for error in the manual process, and, because it was so labour-intensive, long delays were commonplace.

It was Sandy and her team's mission to create a process where assignees could enter their information directly into IBM's system, thus greatly reducing cycle time and cost. This was not as easy to implement as it sounds, because there were many variables that had to be included, calling for a great deal of detail and research.

Not only was her team able to accomplish this goal on time, but the team developed such a good system that IBM decided to consolidate assignee processing into their domestic system, setting Sandy yet another challenge. That consolidation has led to big savings for the computer giant.

She was then asked to take on another difficult task: revamping the tax reconciliation process. When assignees go overseas, they are required to pay both US and foreign taxes, and IBM must ensure that the proper amounts of taxes are paid to both governments. This is complex, and so laborious that until Sandy and her team implemented a new process, there was a backlog of literally hundreds of cases at any one time, making their 'customers', the assignees, frustrated, as well as the employees who had to compile and process this information. This resulted in cost overruns and unnecessary overheads.

Once again, through teamwork and creativity, Sandy succeeded. Although their first efforts involved employees in just one country, Japan, the pilot country had no backlog at the end of the first year, and a 90 per cent customer satisfaction rating. The next step is to integrate France, Hong Kong and Singapore into the new process, and there are plans to expand the system to Germany, Italy and the UK.

How has Sandy achieved such remarkable results?

It began with the team Sandy chose, made up of individuals she knew were enthusiastic and likely to be able to inspire each other. She handpicked from other departments in IBM people she deemed 'change agents' – skilled, open to change, flexible and enthusiastic. She rejected paper-pushers who did not seem to be interested in anything more than bringing home a paycheque.

She also took into consideration the specific skills she needed, and made sure she had the right mix. The project manager was chosen for his technical skills in understanding global tax implications. The team leader's interpersonal skills are such that she can persuade ten IBM executives to set aside three hours for a meeting when necessary. The processor is an account analyst who has both payroll and system experience, and an excellent eye for detail. A skilled writer documents what goes on, and explains in writing how everything works, including the roles and responsibilities of organizations within and outside IBM. Once the team was in place, it was drilled in the motto: 'If one of us succeeds, we all succeed.'

From the very beginning, Sandy established several policies.

No one would ever be penalized or criticized for expressing an opinion or tendering an idea. 'My team members don't mind speaking up,' she says. 'When I recently suggested a goal they felt was too ambitious, they said so, and explained why. We ended up adjusting the goal.' Ironically, the team worked so smoothly that they accomplished what Sandy had originally asked of them – but no one felt pressured to do something they felt was burdensome.

Each employee would be allowed to shine and be recognized by management. 'I'm not afraid to put employees in the limelight and build them up in the eyes of superiors,' says Sandy. 'Often managers aren't interested in building up anyone but themselves, but I generate more team loyalty this way.' At least once a month, Sandy and her team meet face to face with Sandy's boss. She opens the meeting, steps back and lets team members speak. They receive direct feedback, rather than hearing it through a chain of command, and have an opportunity to be recognized for their contributions.

Any employee who could better serve IBM in another capacity would be suggested for promotion, even though it meant leaving a gap in the team. Sandy recently took one of her key members and transferred her to Sandy's boss, because Sandy felt this employee could better serve IBM as a whole in that capacity, as well as gain personal growth. 'I have the attitude that she can help us all succeed by being in that job,' Sandy explained.

Each team member would be seen as an individual, and each individual's needs would be taken into consideration when necessary. When possible, one of Sandy's staff arranges her work schedule so that she can be home by 3.30 p.m. to meet her child's school bus. Sandy lets her come in early, and tries not to schedule team meetings in the late afternoon. Another member of staff who put in excessive hours during the weeks before going to Florida on holiday was supposed to return to work on a Thursday. Sandy told him to take Thursday and Friday off on full pay to thank him for his exceptional efforts in completing work projects, giving him and his family four more days' vacation. 'He made up those two days tenfold,' Sandy said. 'Do I suffer by doing these things? No. Does IBM lose anything? Absolutely not. We all win.'

To keep a mountain of complex information manageable, Sandy relies on Mind Maps. When working on the tax reconciliation projects, she and the team made the 'frustrated customer' the central image, since there was a lot of dissatisfaction from their customers which needed to be corrected. The Mind Map branches dealt with the various sources of that frustration, and possible remedies. The Mind Maps were always brought out during staff meetings, and were added to on a regular basis. 'It was a quick and easy way to remind everyone of what we were doing,' said Sandy, who also brought Mind Maps to meetings with her bosses. 'I could fit on one Mind Map what would ordinarily require a dozen charts.'

Sandy has had a great impact on IBM's bottom line, and is not fearful of committing and delivering results. She has experienced a tremendous amount of personal satisfaction by coaching others to reach their potential. 'I let my people know that they are needed and wanted,' she says. Also, she doesn't want anyone on the team who doesn't want to be a part of it. 'And, you know what? Every time someone gets a promotion and is transferred out, sooner or later I get a call asking if they can come back and work with the team in some capacity.'

Clearly, Sandy knows how to help everyone become a winner. She is a BrainSmart Leader.

Conclusion

Every leader who wants to exert a positive influence on their team members needs to integrate the seven Brain Principles into their daily actions. Building trust and confidence to the point where people will communicate openly is essential to success.

ACTIVITIES

1a. Select an outstanding member of your team and develop a mini public relations programme to inform others about your star performers.

1b. Ask your star performer to do the same thing for someone they view as an outstanding member of their team.

2. List all the people who report to you. Each week write one positive sentence about each person. Review the list with each person every few weeks.

3. Schedule up to a 90-minute meeting with each of your employees to discuss their career goals and how you can be of help.

4. Carry out a time log of where you are spending your time. Analyse your list of activities and see if there are opportunities to teach some of these activities to your staff.

5. Based on the company vision, develop your organizational goals with your team so that they share the same goals.

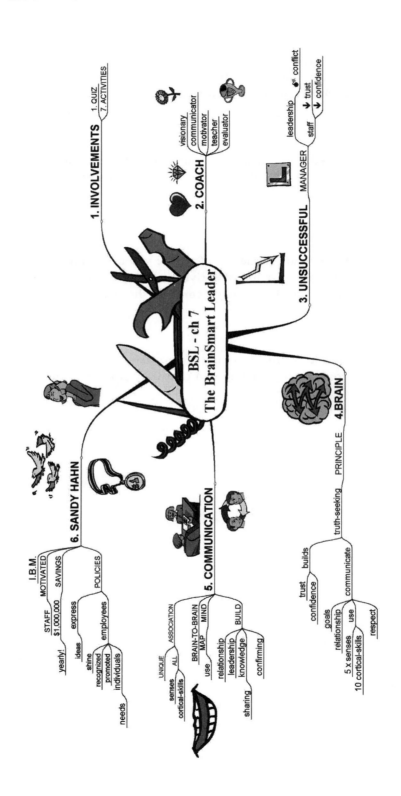

BSL - ch 7
The BrainSmart Leader

1. INVOLVEMENTS
1. QUIZ
7. ACTIVITIES

2. COACH
visionary
communicator
motivator
teacher
evaluator

3. UNSUCCESSFUL
MANAGER
leadership
conflict
staff
trust
confidence

4. BRAIN
PRINCIPLE
truth-seeking
trust
builds
confidence
goals
relationship
communicate
5 x senses
use
10 cortical-skills
respect

5. COMMUNICATION
UNIQUE
ASSOCIATION
senses
ALL
cortical-skills
BRAIN-TO-BRAIN
MAP
MIND
use
relationship
leadership
knowledge
BUILD
sharing
confirming

6. SANDY HAHN
I.B.M.
MOTIVATED
STAFF
SAVINGS
$1,000,000
POLICIES
yearly!
express
ideas
shine
recognized
employees
promoted
individuals
needs

8 PEOPLE POWER

Quiz

1. Do you think it is important to continuously improve and add to your skills/knowledge? Yes/No

2. Have you ever studied how the human brain works? Yes/No

3. Do you share your ideas with others? Yes/No

4. Do you believe there is a business reason for understanding your thinking? Yes/No

5. Should a value be shown in a company's annual report on human or Intellectual Capital? Yes/No

6. Is it a good idea to withhold your knowledge within a company? Yes/No

7. Is there a limit to the amount of knowledge a human brain can store? Yes/No

8. Is there a correlation between income and vocabulary? Yes/No

9. Are there companies that include people as an asset in their annual report? Yes/No

10. Does the brain by its very nature seek out new knowledge? Yes/No

SCORING

Score two points for 'Yes' to all questions, except score two points for 'No' to questions 6 and 7.

If you scored over 18 points, you know how to manage people. This chapter will help you fine-tune your management skills. If you scored 18 or less, this chapter will show you how to unleash the limitless creative potential of your workforce.

Overview

Enthusiastic and excited people consistently generate ideas and new ways of doing things, but their ability to do so can be limited by their self-imposed limits or how you communicate thoughts and messages to them. We've all seen teams of athletes draw on the diverse skills of each member to achieve success. To communicate effectively, you must first understand the thinking skills you possess, and the way you process information.

People power: managing change

SKILLS INVENTORY

Your mind possesses a natural stock of knowledge and beliefs that it has developed over the years which governs how you behave and react today. These behaviours are developed and reinforced by your environment and your responses to it. As new events in your life occur, your brain associates, connects and files the new information in your database of knowledge and beliefs. Memories and experiences are interlinked, somewhat like the roads and highways on a map. If you travel the same path more than once, you learn most of the bumps and turns on the road.

Think of a childhood experience when you first began to build a new skill, such as speaking, writing or playing a sport. Do you remember gaining confidence in your new skill? How did that affect your eagerness to practise and continue learning? Now contrast this feeling with the first time you believed you were unable to learn a new skill like drawing, writing or memorizing multiplication tables. From childhood, many of us have been taught that we just weren't born with the aptitude for certain skills, and because we were not born with them, there was no possibility we could ever master them through hard work and practice. We were encouraged to identify and believe in our limitations. This belief becomes a self-fulfilling prophecy, because it causes us to short-circuit our brain's success mechanism and closes a road in our mental network of skills. This means we fail to develop our full range of cortical skills, which in turn reduces our ability to be creative.

The truth is that our brain has the ability to learn *any* skill, and open *any* path, if we are interested, find the right model to follow, have access to good coaching, and practise.

To fully develop your brain, you must continue to add to your stock of skills, and to develop those skills you need to improve. For example, if your profession relies on skills that are predominantly left-cortex, such as accounting, work on developing several of your right-cortex skills, like music or drawing. If your profession requires skills that are predominantly right-cortex, such as art, work on developing left-brain skills, like logic or foreign languages.

Why should you try to improve seemingly 'irrelevant' skills? Because when the brain is working well, there is constant communication between the left and right sides of the brain's cortex. The two sides of the brain working together in harmony generate ideas and natural creativity.

It is not surprising to learn that innovators like Einstein or Disney developed each of the ten cortical skills to a high degree. Albert Einstein is considered by many to be the greatest scientist of the twentieth century. We are all familiar with his scientific ability from his development of the theory of relativity, but it was Einstein's vivid imagination that allowed him to understand the relationship between mass and energy, and the interdependence of space and time. Einstein claimed that his first insight into the theory of relativity came from a daydream in which he imagined he was riding a light beam towards the end of the universe. To his astonishment, at the end of his imaginary journey he had returned to his starting point!

On a somewhat different level of achievement, Walt Disney is well known for his colourful imagination, his storytelling ability and his creation of the cartoon characters Mickey Mouse and Donald Duck. He could also pay intense attention to detail. During construction of Disneyland, he guided Disney 'Imagineers' in applying scientific precision and meticulous attention to the smallest details to create attractions which were designed to stimulate both the left and right cortices of the brains of park visitors.

As cortical skill development takes place, your brain possesses an infinite ability to link and associate new ideas with existing knowledge. Any limitations on generating new ideas stem from self-imposed belief systems. Regardless of whether these limits were developed on our own or with the assistance of a parent, teacher or coach, we have the power to decide to remove them.

A common misconception is that our brain has a finite amount of storage for new ideas and knowledge: if we use valuable brain space to learn skills which do not immediately apply to our profession, we run the risk of 'running out of room' for more important information. The reality is that the more we learn, the easier it becomes for us to associate and link new knowledge – in effect, our brain expands. As we remove roadblocks that have been placed in the highways of our brains, we discover new roads that have yet to be travelled. Your level of skill mastery determines how fast you can navigate these roads, but they can be travelled by anyone.

INPUT DEVICES

The human brain has more than 10 trillion cells called *neurons*, each one made up of a sending branch called an *axon* and receiving branches called *dendrites*. When an axon sends a message, it can connect with up to 100,000 adjoining cells. Each cell that is connected with the first neuron can connect with another 100,000 neurons. This linking and connecting of cells creates memory traces and thought patterns. With so many possible combinations available, how many unique thoughts and traces do you think the brain can create?

When you combine the unlimited biological potential of the brain with the seven Brain Principles outlined in Chapter 3, you discover that the information you input into your brain dictates the direction of your own thoughts. This will either provide the resources to overcome obstacles that block our journey to success, or else the reasons why we really can't do something. To take advantage of this, you must first understand the GIGG model more clearly (see page 32).

Start by thinking about how you have defined success, and whether or not you have placed limits on your definition because of some incorrect beliefs. Remember that the brain is truth-seeking, and will act on what it believes to be true. At times you may want to question how and why you accept some of your beliefs to be true. Write down reasons why you believe them to be so; revalidate or question those reasons, and perhaps discard them, and realize that they may not be appropriate in the present (for example, perhaps your brother told you years ago that you would never be an accountant or be able to add up numbers).

So how do you begin to direct your brain to overcome barriers and limitations? The first step is to examine closely the type of information you are putting into your brain. As explained in Chapter 3, your brain takes all new information, and links and associates it with existing knowledge. This information becomes the starting point for creating new ideas, and acts as an investment in the development of your Intellectual Capital and people power. To maximize the return on this investment, you must ensure that the type and quality of your input are consistent with your individual goals. Some typical sources of new information are TV, newspapers, professional journals and the people with whom you interact on a daily basis. Although you will not always have direct control over everything you store in your long-term memory, you need to be aware that the quality of the information you take in determines how well your skills inventory grows. Even your own thoughts can act as inputs, influencing whether your brain is willing to accept the value of developing new skills.

Your brain follows the model of GIGG, and you ultimately control whether the first 'G' will represent 'Garbage' ('Garbage in garbage grows') or 'Good' ('Good in, good grows'). If your inputs currently fall into the 'Garbage' category, you can make the necessary changes to convert them into 'Good'. Your brain unconsciously uses the mimic principle to model and duplicate the behaviour and mannerisms of your associates. If these behaviours include cynicism and a lack of positive thinking, your brain may accept this input as true, and thus programme itself to fail. If you combine negative thinking with additional 'Garbage' inputs, your brain will programme itself to fail very quickly and effectively.

It is natural to want to vent problems and frustrations. Co-workers experiencing the same frustrations will relate to each other easily, and will strengthen these feelings further. The combination of 'Garbage' inputs and the mimic principle could cause you to fall in with the consensus before you realize your thinking has changed. Without even being aware, you may have built a roadblock, which obstructs your creativity. Whether you are a manager or junior member of staff, you must be sensitive to the input you receive and that you provide to others. The quality of your thoughts will determine whether a team of creative, excited thinkers or a group of negative, apathetic whiners surrounds you. You choose the direction of the thoughts you generate each day.

New information combined with existing knowledge keeps your brain alive and generating new ideas. This provides the fuel to keep you moving in the direction of your goals. Some of the resources you need to develop improved input are probably within reach right now. With a little persistence (Brain Principle 7), you can usually find a model representing your goals for your brain to mimic (Brain Principle 3). An excellent source of information is to read a book on a subject which interests you. Feeding your brain positive, useful information helps strengthen your mental powers.

Another way of gaining information is to ask questions of someone who has already mastered a skill you wish to improve or acquire. Our experiences have continually demonstrated that the most successful people in a company are least likely to be asked by their peers to share the secrets of their success. Sometimes our ego keeps us from asking our closest allies for help. People are usually eager to talk about their triumphs, and enjoy the experience of sharing with others how they achieved it.

Tony Dottino saw an example of this tendency when he met an artist at the Metropolitan Museum of Art. Tony was interested in learning more about art, and asked the artist what he was working on. During the next hour, the artist passionately described how he drew his paintings using various tools. He explained how he studied and visualized his subjects with far more attention to detail than untrained eyes. The one-hour art lesson enabled Tony to view all paintings from a new perspective, because his brain had developed new relationships and connections to an existing interest.

THE IMPORTANCE OF LISTENING

Listening is an integral part of communication. As we listen to other people speak, we often start forming opinions about what they say before they are finished ('It's not going to work, it's a terrible idea, and they don't know what they're talking about!') By doing so, we've deprived our brain of the motivation to listen, to explore these possibilities and create new ideas.

Likewise, if a person's opinion is in the minority in a group meeting, we tend to ignore it, treating them as a misfit, as 'not part of the team', whereas they may be presenting missing information that could lead to creative solutions.

When listening to others express their ideas, listen to gain understanding, build compassion and communicate your own point of view without antagonizing others.

Learning to manage change

How do you take all of this information and knowledge and apply it to effect change in your business life? Learning to manage change has become the greatest challenge in many companies. Because of the

BrainSmart!

Here are some techniques to improve the quality of your own input and of the input of those around you:

- Remember the concept of 'Good In, Good Grows'.
- Avoid negative reinforcement of ideas. They cause brains to cultivate scepticism and hinder their ability to generate solutions for existing problems.
- Ask questions of people who excel at skills you wish to mimic.
- Be aware of the quality of sources of information that provide input into your brain.
- Invest in the development of Intellectual Capital.
- Consider new sources of information, such as books, the Internet, college classes, or professional training.

acceleration in technology and the increasing sophistication of customers, even the largest companies have had to try to become nimble and flexible. Despite the latest technology available, many companies still find it a struggle to implement change rather than just react to it. Why is this the case? To answer that question, you must first understand how we think when we learn, and how we develop new habits.

LEARNING TO LEARN

You are probably familiar with the term 'learning curve', which is used to describe the process of improving a skill through practice and experience. We sometimes refer to it as the 'change curve', because people learn as they are changing. If you had to draw a typical learning/change curve, what would it look like? Most people draw a curve that resembles the one in Figure 8.1.

In fact, every learning curve that people have drawn at our request looks similar to the one shown in Figure 8.1, the only variation being the gradient of the curve. Yet this diagram is inaccurate.

What would the consequences be if you found that the learning curve of the human brain looks nothing like the curve in this example? What if you discovered that learning new skills does not occur evenly over time, but instead has many peaks and troughs?

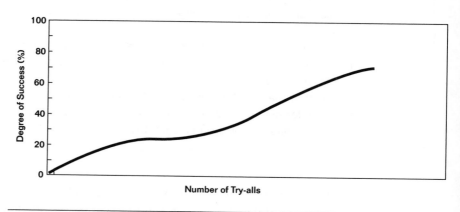

What do you think the learning curve of the human brain looks like?

Figure 8.1   The common idea of the learning curve

The Learning/Change Curve is Not Smooth.

Although your brain is constantly learning, the integration of new knowledge into your existing knowledge base does not occur evenly. In your own experience, have you felt that despite practising a new skill, your mastery of that skill undergoes occasional performance dips? Have you ever felt that a skill you have already mastered is deteriorating? Well, the good news is that both of these occurrences are perfectly normal!

Figure 8.2 gives a much more accurate representation of what the learning process of your brain looks like.

You may have already noticed some important differences:

- **The learning process is not smooth** – Your improvement in a skill will involve many peaks and troughs. There will be times when your improvement in a skill will occur rapidly. There will be other times where your mastery regresses, and you will struggle just to maintain the status quo. Both of these experiences are normal, and both occur regularly during the learning process.

- **The learning process contains many troughs** – You may have noticed that the curve contains many downturns, and at least one instance where the skill mastery is not much greater than at the very beginning of the learning process. We have illustrated those points on Figure 8.2 with a drawing of a 'big black hole'.

What normally happens at the big black hole?

Try to remember the last time you were practising to strengthen a new skill. Do you recall a time when you felt you had hit rock bottom? What type of self-talk did you give yourself when that happened? What things do you think most people say to themselves at this time?

Our surveys have revealed that the worst (and most common) self-talk at this point is: 'I can't do this! I give up!'

Now imagine that you understand that the learning process contains many periods where progress in skill acquisition is flat or reverses itself. Ask someone who plays golf if they have ever experienced this. Would your self-talk be different if you believed those downturns were both normal and temporary?

At this point, your most helpful self-talk would be: 'How interesting! How fascinating! What can I learn from this?'

When you believe that learning is constant and smooth, any failure to progress must be perceived negatively. This encourages negative thinking and self-recrimination, because *any* slippage, however minor, is seen as an indication of failure. Regression is viewed as failure, which in turn associates itself with other thoughts of failure. Your thinking will become more pessimistic, because each of those negative associations will trigger other associations. You will unleash a self-doubting, self-defeating cascade of thoughts that will reinforce the belief 'I can't do that', and give up (an example of Garbage In, Garbage Grows).

If you accept that learning naturally occurs in uneven bursts, temporary deterioration is not catastrophic. You will no longer view it as an indictment of your own ability, a failure, but as a normal, expected event. This separates the emotional reaction and fear of failure from the event, and allows your brain to deal with the issue without any negative thoughts.

Picture the contrast between these two outlooks on learning and events. Consider the impact that will have on you, your organization and its view

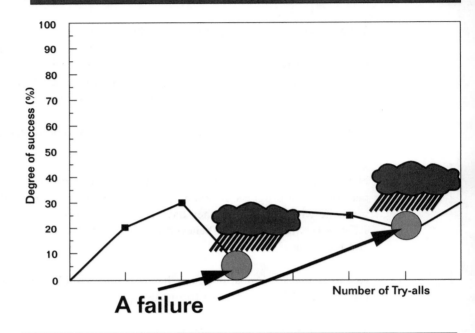

What are some of the typical responses to failure?

Figure 8.2 The true learning/change curve

of 'failure'. Is failure seen as a bump on the road to success? Or is failure viewed as a dead end, or a mistake that deserves to be punished? How your company regards failure will greatly influence whether or not you have a dynamic, innovative organization. (For a detailed treatment of this theme, see Tony Buzan's video *If at first . . .*, produced by Charthouse.)

LEARNING TO CHANGE BEHAVIOUR

You are now ready to combine the information and knowledge you have learned in this chapter and use it to effect a change in your life by altering a behaviour or habit.

Let's assume that you have a behaviour or habit that you would like to change (such as arriving to work late each morning). If you wanted to develop self-talk that would maximize your chance of changing this behaviour, what would it be?

Your brain will take any self-talk that is entered into it, and associate it with existing thoughts. If you reprimand yourself each morning after you are already late, saying to yourself, 'I won't arrive late tomorrow,' your brain will emphasize the phrase 'arrive late tomorrow'. This self-talk will actually increase your probability of being late tomorrow, and other days in the future! Your goal must always be positive, and must include the outcome you hope to achieve. In this instance, it should include something like 'arrive at work on time' or 'become more punctual'.

However, if you develop positive self-talk that is factually incorrect, such as 'I am someone who arrives to work on time' when you are often late, your brain will reject this input. You will recall from Chapter 3 that the brain is truth-seeking (Brain Principle 6). If it is fed information that it knows is inaccurate, it will discard that information.

On the other hand, if you develop positive self-talk that is factually correct but is not related to time/action, your brain will accept the information, but not act upon it. For example, if your self-talk is 'I will arrive at work on time', that statement may be true, but it is based in the future. Since this statement is not based in the present, your brain will not act to make it true. The behaviour change will be left to occur 'later', and later will always be redefined so that the behaviour never changes.

If none of these approaches will work, what self-talk *should* you use to be effective? Your input must be:

- **positive** – stating the goal as a positive outcome
- **factually correct** – not an expression of what you would like the truth to be
- **in the present tense** – so that your brain is moved *immediately* into action and continues.

We recommend telling yourself: 'I am becoming punctual.' That statement meets all the requirements above, and more importantly, it takes into account your learning curve. What if you begin repeating this phrase to yourself today, and tomorrow you are late for work. Would the above self-talk still be correct? Yes, because you are in the *process* of becoming punctual. Since the learning process is uneven, it allows for events such as arriving at work after your specified time. You still allow yourself opportunities to learn from the occasions where you do not meet your goal on a given day, but you avoid the frustration and negative thinking that accompany viewing the event as a 'failure'. Persisting with this self-talk will move you along the road to success, until your brain has reprogrammed itself to be punctual.

Consider your organization's views about change. Is it nurturing, saying 'You can do it!', or is there cynicism and resignation when newly defined goals are not met immediately? Are goals phrased so that they are consistent with how the brain learns to modify its behaviour? Are the goals phrased positively? For example, if you have a 10 per cent error rate in a process, will your goal be to lower the error rate to, say, 5 per cent? It would be more effective to state the goal in terms of the desired success rate – 95 per cent.

Are your goals in line with current reality? Does the executive team tell itself, 'We are a world-class provider of information services', when the reality is that you are struggling to hold onto your existing customer base? Your goals must be positive, but they must also be honest.

Finally, are your goals based in the present, therefore requiring immediate action, or are they phrased so that action may be delayed until the future? Do you have goals which say, 'We will become the industry leader in XYZ', or are they defined as 'We are in the process of becoming the industry leader in XYZ.' Even that small distinction will affect the chances of your organization achieving its goal.

Leadership profile: Mary Vasso-Ortega

In 1996, Mary Vasso-Ortega was handed the professional challenge of a lifetime when she was appointed the plant re-engineering expert for her employer, a major American West Coast manufacturing company. She was charged with raising employee morale and significantly improving one of eleven aspects of inferior plant performance – materials inventory accuracy.

The company had downsized, eliminating all its long-serving managers. Everyone remaining had been shuffled into jobs they had never done before and weren't sure how to do, and nobody was happy.

Several years earlier, Mary had taken the Mental Literacy workshop to access her natural intelligence and creativity. In the workshop Mary learned the model of the brain as a success-driven mechanism. She was taught to look at every problem as a fascinating learning opportunity, and to believe that if she could imagine it, she could do it:

> I learned a fresh perspective for dealing with failure. Whenever a student was confronted with what seemed to be an intractable business problem, we learned to say, 'How interesting. How fascinating. What can we learn from this?' We learned to look at mistakes not as failures, but as events from which we could learn to do things better. Since failure was an event, not an outcome, by applying Brain Principles properly, success was not only likely, but *inevitable*!

> We also learned that increased intelligence and creativity were unleashed whenever we tapped into the intrinsic motivation of people. If we could make work more 'fun', we would generate enthusiasm and excitement, which would in turn fuel creativity. Creativity could also be increased by increasing the number of cortical skills that were used regularly.

Mary believed that was true, but it was going to take all the belief she could muster – not to mention a lot of creativity and hard work – to transform the plant's substandard performance.

TEAMWORK

Mary became involved in Small Group Improvement Teams. She was a member of the SGIA (Small Group Improvement Activity) Steering Committee, and was a member of an SGIA advertising and marketing team.

Her task was to persuade employees to volunteer to become part of teams of six to eight people devoted to solving a particular problem. The corporate office did not want to steamroll anyone into these teams, as they knew the teams would be more effective if participants were enthusiastic.

For months before Mary's arrival, the company had been trying to put together just 20 teams from among its 1 000 employees, but it was 'like pulling teeth'. Most people just wanted to go to work, bring home a paycheque and let 'somebody else' tackle the problems, so Mary faced a difficult problem:

> Sitting in my apartment one evening, thinking of the challenge

ahead in reaching a plant goal of 20 active SGIA teams, the question came to me: 'What would motivate employees to join teams and get involved?' Efforts thus far had only produced a handful of teams. In the background I could hear the song 'YMCA' on the radio. Suddenly, the answer to the question came to me – in the form of music!

As I listened to the song, a familiar rush of energy and excitement returned. If this music could form a positive and uplifting association for me, it could very well affect others the same way. Before I went to bed, I placed another question in my brain – how to come up with lyrics to the song? By the time morning came, I was surprised and delighted to realize that I had those lyrics.

Full of enthusiasm and bursting to share my idea, I actually sang 'YMCA' with SGIA lyrics to a few of my peers that morning at the Steering Committee meeting. Speaking from past experience, I stressed the value of creativity in attracting employee attention and involvement. Throughout the day, when the opportunity arose, I shared the song:

> Hey there! Take a look at your job!
> I said you there! Are there problems to solve?
> You can do that through an SGIA.
> It can start you off on your way.
>
> Once you get involved with a team,
> You'll see problems aren't as big as they seem.
> You can solve them with the help of your friends,
> We can get it done together!
>
> SGIA, it's fun to be on an SGIA.
> You'll learn everything you need to be on a team,
> You can have your voice heard today!
> SGIA, it's great to be on an SGIA.
> For us all to succeed it is *you* that we need,
> So get yourself involved right away!

The feedback Mary received was mixed. Some thought this approach was a bit too far out, while others saw its potential. 'I knew it could work, and suggested making it into a music video,' she said.

While the decision about what to do with it was debated, Mary's three-month assignment with the company expired. Homesick, Mary decided to leave the company and return to the West Coast. Little did she know, however, that her 'far out' creativity would have a major impact on her old company.

Four months after leaving, Mary received a phone call. The voice on the other end said, 'Mary, I have something for you to hear!' As she listened, she heard the familiar SGIA words, put to music. She was told that with the help of a few 'inspired' team members, the video had been created. It debuted on SGIA Day, a day designated to celebrate and promote small group improvement teams. The celebration took place in the corporate cafeteria, with employees from all shifts.

When the video was played, employee reaction was electric. The song was also voice-mailed to each plant profit centre manager. The next day, people flooded the switchboard with calls requesting copies. The result? Over 150 employees signed up to become involved in 30 teams. The goal of 20 SGIA teams that once seemed insurmountable was surpassed practically overnight, and Mary had become a legend who is still talked about even today.

After leaving her long-time employer, Mary decided to embark on a business of her own, and today is a professional job coach, still employing many of the wonderful lessons she learned at her old job: 'I know the delightful "gift" of creativity resides within each of us, and I've seen firsthand its power in motivating, inspiring and educating,' she said. 'Now I hope to continue teaching it to others.'

Conclusion

We live in a world that perceives technology as the driving force for change. We should remember that it is *people* who create, improve and apply technology to bring about this change. No technology would exist without the applied creativity of people. Today, people exchange much more information at higher speeds than ever before, thanks to such tools as the Internet, fax machines and cellular telephones. However, we need to be constantly alert to the need for the human brain to be in control, supported by the marvels of modern technology.

ACTIVITIES

1. List the topics that your superior has discussed with you over the last six months regarding your personal development. What is your plan for implementation?

2. Write a letter to someone complimenting them on their success.
   Who:
   What:

3. Introduce yourself to one new person each week, and list five interesting things you learned about each person.

4. Join a volunteer group and take a leadership role.

5. When returning home at the end of the day, let your first five minutes of conversation be about 'good things' that have happened to each family member during the day.

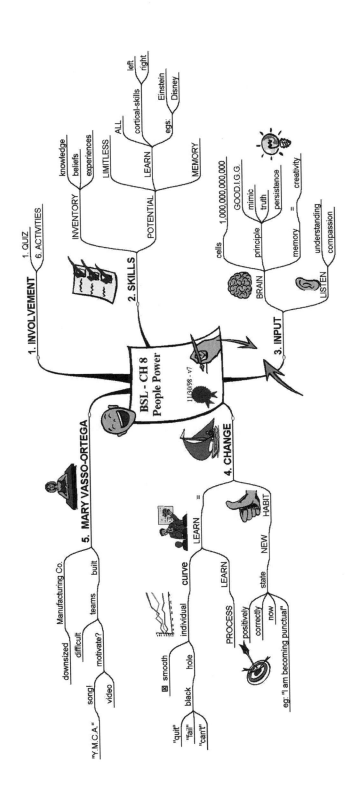

9 MANAGING INFORMATION I

Quiz

1. Are you up to date with all the information you need for peak job performance?   Yes/No

2. Is there an area of knowledge where you consider yourself as an expert?   Yes/No

3. Do you avoid sharing knowledge as a protective device for job security?   Yes/No

4. Do you believe that you can make a greater knowledge contribution than you are presently making?   Yes/No

5. Do you think that knowledge and information are the ultimate competitive advantage?   Yes/No

6. Are you using computer technology to access information?   Yes/No

7. Do you know how to use knowledge and information to inform and educate others?   Yes/No

8. Do you have a method for capturing all your daily ideas?   Yes/No

9. Do you communicate with experts in your field?   Yes/No

10. Do you document your customer findings into a knowledge base?   Yes/No

SCORING

Score two points for 'Yes' to all questions, except score two points for 'No' to question 3.

If you scored over 18 points, you already understand the power of information and this chapter gives you suggestions for becoming a knowledge power-house. If you scored less than 18 points, this chapter will help you become an effective knowledge worker.

Overview

We take in data through our five senses, and from this data we derive information and form our perception of reality. This chapter looks at this complete process – from raw data to information, and finally, knowledge.

Data, information and knowledge

The life-blood of any business is data, information and knowledge.

No, that's not just three ways of saying the same thing. Each term means something different, and the distinctions are important. For our purposes, we will define the terms as follows:

- *Data* consists of raw facts.
- Data that has been organized becomes *information*.
- Information that can be used to create something of value becomes *knowledge*.
- Knowledge that is applied becomes *experience* – and finally *wisdom*.

In most of this chapter, we will be discussing information. When we are talking about data or knowledge, we will make the distinction clear.

The problem with information is that we never seem to have exactly what we need when we need it. We may have too much or too little, and sometimes, even when we have the right amount, we discover that the wrong people have it, not those who can put it to use.

All too often in this information age, it turns out that the information we don't have is vital.

A second problem is that even when we have the information, we don't always turn it into knowledge – we don't use it to create solutions for ourselves and our customers. We don't have to look far to find examples. They are all around us.

Too little knowledge is a dangerous thing

Take the case of American Airlines. The company had accumulated a vast amount of information on the best way to put together a holiday package.

While this was important and valuable, the company saw the information only as an adjunct to its real business: flying people from place to place at reasonable fares.

Company officials were surprised to discover that many of its customers were more interested in the holiday information than they were in the low airfares the airline had introduced to win price wars. The information was available, but was initially undervalued. It hadn't been turned into knowledge.

Or consider the case of the graphics company that frequently surveyed a particular customer, asking typical questions about the customer's satisfaction with the level of support being provided, the timeliness of the services, and the colour schemes shown on charts.

When the company eventually asked the customer another series of questions involving some proposed improvements, it was shocked to discover that the customer was planning to invest in its own graphics technology and do everything in-house. The graphics company had been dutifully gathering data, but it was the wrong data. It simply hadn't been asking the right questions, so its efforts to improve its customer service were fruitless.

Fortunately, the graphics company discovered its error in time to make the changes necessary to salvage the account. It proposed that the two companies work together to meet their future needs. It pointed out to the customer that it had a great deal of experience in preparing reports and presentations and other graphics-oriented materials, and an encyclopaedic knowledge of the process that the customer could not quickly or easily acquire. The customer agreed, and they developed a new working arrangement.

While information is valuable, the wrong kind of information can be worse than useless – it can be disastrous.

Let's take another example. A manufacturing company was startled to discover that customers were unhappy because of its shipping policy. To expedite deliveries, the manufacturer was in the habit of shipping whatever part of the order was available immediately, and the rest when it became available later. Company officials assumed that quicker delivery would please their customers. However, a work team discovered that customers viewed incomplete deliveries negatively. They called them 'split orders', and disliked them intensely.

The salespeople, who dealt with customers every day, were aware of this attitude, but this information had never been shared with staff in the manufacturing, shipping and scheduling departments. Once the appropriate company officials were made aware of the problem, they were able to modify their procedures accordingly.

In this case, staff withheld information, however inadvertently, from their managers, preventing the company using it to create something of value for the customer, but the same problem can happen in reverse, with managers failing to share vital information with their employees.

In one company, maintenance workers were doing their best to patch up some old equipment to make it last to the end of the calendar year, when they believed it was due to be scrapped. This perception surfaced during a workshop designed to explore operating problems. The maintenance department questioned whether it was cost-effective to carry out so much work on equipment that would soon be redundant. The company president was astonished – rather than scrapping the machines, the company intended to increase production of the goods they made by 200 per cent.

Because the available information hadn't been shared with those who needed it, management and workers were operating at cross purposes.

One common factor in most of these problems is poor communication of data/information. Communication is one of the most powerful and least expensive tools you can use to gather information about your internal and external customers, so it is surprising that so few companies use it effectively.

At any given time, a tremendous amount of information is being communicated within a company, or between the company and its customers. Too often, however, as in some of the examples we discussed earlier, the communication is between the wrong parties, or the relevant information is not passed on. Frequently, the people who could most benefit from the information are the last to receive it.

Usually, the lack of communication is unintentional – the result of poor management structures, or a perception by one person or department that everyone else already knows the information – but sometimes the lack of communication is deliberate, the result of a natural tendency to avoid being the messenger bearing bad news, particularly if previous bearers of bad news weren't well received.

Another information-sharing problem is frequently seen in companies that have made many workers redundant. Very often when companies downsize, there is a tendency among the remaining workers to stop sharing information: they feel that if they possess information that others don't, their job security will be enhanced. As a result, the company isn't able to make full use of its resources. The creativity that is sparked by the sharing of information is lost. In addition, there are increasing gaps in the information available, which are too often plugged by guesses and wrong assumptions.

The problems associated with this poor communication are obvious, but imagine what it would be like if we could communicate so effectively that all our combined information and knowledge were focused on the needs of the customer. That is exactly what we are striving for. The possibilities are almost beyond imagination. Since everyone in a company has a different set of information and knowledge stored in their brains, the interactions between them open up endless opportunities for new insights. As information is shared, our brain links new inputs to millions of different associations that perhaps had never been considered before.

The challenge is this: find ways to take all this information in, to do so faster, to retain it longer, to communicate it, and to use it to create new ideas and solutions. We will discuss this further in Chapter 10.

You can have too much of a good thing

Until now, we have been considering the problem of insufficient information, but a growing problem today is that very often we don't have too little data – we have too much.

We live in an information age. We are surrounded by it. We receive information not only from traditional sources, such as newspapers, magazines, radio and TV, inter-office communications and our customers, but from new sources, such as the Internet, particularly e-mail and the World Wide Web.

E-mail alone has dramatically increased the communication workload most of us face each day. Some people receive more than 200 e-mail messages a day. When one pathologist returned to his office after three weeks away, he discovered 1 500 e-mail messages waiting for him. The Internet's World Wide Web contains millions of sites maintained by individuals, universities and colleges, and businesses ranging in size from individual florist shops to international corporate giants. You can find information about nearly everything on the Web: an abundance of it; too much of it.

This information overload leads to frustration, confusion, and sometimes total inability to make essential decisions. It can also lead to emotional and physical health problems. A recent survey of 1 313 managers in the UK, USA, Australia, Hong Kong and Singapore, *Dying for Information? An Investigation into the Effects of Information Overload in the UK and Worldwide*, revealed that one in four of them felt that the glut of information is so overwhelming that it causes them to suffer mental anguish, and even physical illness. The report found that as a result of the stress caused by information overload:

- 33 per cent of managers reported increased tension with colleagues that had led to decreased job satisfaction,
- 62 per cent felt that their personal relationships had suffered,
- 43 per cent thought that important decisions were being delayed, and
- 33 per cent suffered ill health – this figure rose to 43 per cent among senior managers.

Nearly half the managers surveyed saw the Internet as the main cause of information overload, and more than 80 per cent cited the rapid increase of internal communications within companies, and communications with customers and suppliers.

The Internet's main functions – e-mail, news groups and the World Wide Web – each have implications for the information overload problem.

The problem with electronic mail is that it is too easy. You can compose and send an e-mail in seconds, but you may spend hours regretting it. E-mail encourages facile rather than thoughtful communication, and quantity rather than quality. Moreover, it appears to demand an immediate response. In the past, managers who received letters requiring a great deal of thought might let them sit in their in-tray for days while mentally composing a response. When they receive an e-mail message, on the other hand, they feel compelled to answer within hours.

E-mail, like letters, memos and faxes, can create another problem, because it is stripped of all the cues we absorb, mostly unconsciously, in face-to-face conversation: the tone of voice, smiles, frowns and raised eyebrows that frequently communicate more than the words being spoken. The result is that the recipient may misinterpret the sender's intentions, and that in turn may lead to a further exchange of e-mails or notes to clarify what was meant and to soothe hurt feelings.

The problem with news groups is the relatively poor quality of the information available in them. Anyone can join in a discussion in a news group, whether or not they have anything useful to say or any special knowledge of the subject matter. Yet true experts also post messages in news groups, and they can provide invaluable information. Separating the wheat from the chaff is a monumental problem.

The problem with the World Wide Web is similar. Anyone in the world with access to the necessary technology can set up a Web page. The Web sites available range from university-run pages about serious problems such as global warming to product information pages for giant corporations to pictures of someone's pet goldfish.

The difficulty of evaluating information gathered from the Internet is illustrated by an incident in the summer of 1997, when Kurt Vonnegut's commencement address at Massachusetts Institute of Technology touched the hearts of many people, and it spread around the world at the speed of light via the Internet. Someone would receive a copy of the speech and immediately send copies of it to several friends, many of whom would then pass it on to others. The only problem was: it wasn't a speech, it wasn't by Vonnegut, and it wasn't delivered at MIT.

The 'speech' was a copy of an article written by *Chicago Tribune* newspaper columnist Mary Schmich in the form of a mock commencement address. Someone had made a copy of it and, either by accident or design, misidentified the author. It fooled many people, including Vonnegut's wife.

Nothing on the Internet – whether in a news group, e-mail or a Web site – can be taken at face value. This applies to all information, wherever you obtain it. It is vital to evaluate it by applying common sense, and then cross-checking it with other sources. When using the Internet as a source of information, the same rules apply as do to any other form of research. You should always:

- Find out the source of the information.
- Find out why the information is being made available (the author may have ulterior motives).
- Apply common sense (for instance, if a Web site offers a perpetual motion machine for sale, you might be wise to be sceptical).
- Cross-check everything with at least two other sources.

It is not only new resources like the Internet that raise the possibility of information overload, however. In any type of group bound together by a common goal, everyone involved contributes their own unique database of information. As information is shared, our brains link new input to millions of different associations that perhaps had never been considered before. But here again, we are faced with the possibility of information overload.

Stating the problem is the easy part. Is there anything that can be done about lack of information and information overload? Do the new advances in our understanding of the way our minds work bring us any closer to a solution? The answer is 'Yes, but . . .'. The 'but' means that it is going to take some work.

The problem is this: how can we absorb all the information we are flooded with every day, filter out what we need, disseminate it within our organizations, and use it to produce the products or services that our customers need?

There are several tools, several approaches we can use to do exactly that. For example, we can learn filtering skills, learn to read faster and more comprehensively, learn to use our memories better, increase our creativity and learn to use Mind Mapping to manage data.

We will examine these and other coping strategies in Chapter 10, and will discover how some companies have learned to make the best use of some remarkable new tools.

Leadership profile: *Jim Kalinowski, British Airways USA*

Jim Kalinowski is a master at turning data into information and knowledge – a skill that has helped his airline gain a competitive advantage in the USA.

Kalinowski, British Airways' Regional Marketing Manager for the Eastern USA, took data about airline bookings and converted it into knowledge, then created a new approach to the compensation travel agents receive.

In the past, airlines relied heavily on travel agents to sell their products and services, but over the past five years, airlines have shifted aggressively to selling directly to the consumer. On the business (non-leisure) side, direct selling is conducted through relationships with corporations in which a purchase agreement is entered into. On the leisure side, direct selling is achieved through relationships with cruise and tour operators which require air transportation as part of their product offering. The consumer is also reached through advertising and promotions designed to attract travellers to the airline. These cases require no additional selling, and result in increased agency bookings. That's not to say that travel agents don't sell or direct passengers to one airline or another – some do. Even with the direct sales and marketing efforts of the airlines, many passengers rely on the guidance of their agent to help them to make a decision. Airlines such as British Airways rely on them as well: primarily to distribute tickets, but also as an extension of their sales force. But how can airlines tell which agents are just distributing tickets and which are actively promoting and selling their products?

Until 1995, travel agents in the USA used to receive on average about 10 per cent commission on both domestic and international airline tickets, plus additional incentives in many cases, usually based on volume performance. The first reduction in commissions came on domestic tickets, when Delta Airlines capped the amount paid to an agent issuing a domestic airline ticket at $50 for a round trip and $25 for one-way. Most airlines followed this lead. In the second half of 1997, United Airlines cut the commission on international tickets to 8 per cent. Most airlines followed with similar reductions. These moves demoralized the travel agents who saw these changes as a cost-cutting exercise and an attack on their livelihood.

British Airways USA was not interested in cost-cutting, but rather in maximizing their return on investment. For two years, British Airways battled to change the industry-standard commissions. The airline needed to take more responsibility for promoting and selling its products. The commission paid to travel agents in general was in many cases an ineffective investment. It was time to redirect that money to agents that were really promoting and selling British Airways, and to in-house direct marketing campaigns designed to attract passengers to their flights.

No matter how other airlines responded or what pressures were exerted by the travel agent, British Airways USA held its ground. It was able to do this because of the confidence it had in itself and in what its data was telling it – data that had been analysed in a variety of ways, including return-on-investment models, agency-sensitivity models and best-case/worst-case scenario models.

British Airways USA used the knowledge gained from this analysis to create a plan based on two core concepts: to pay a travel agent a fair fee for booking and issuing a ticket on its behalf, and to pay more for improved sales performance. A totally different compensation structure was created, calculated according to a formula that takes into account how actively a travel agency is supporting British Airways. Thanks to the data analysis and the Agency Share Ratios model created by Kalinowski, British Airways USA can judge whether a particular travel agent is selling what the airline considers its natural share of tickets. An agency that sells more than this quota is rewarded as a selling agent, an agency that sells less than the quota is paid solely as a distribution agent and receives a distribution fee, and agents that sell aggressively on behalf of British Airways can earn additional commission.

Most travel agents felt that British Airways' compensation system was more equitable than the competition's, although many were unhappy that sales volume was no longer the main criterion.

What constitutes a fair share in British Airways' view? Kalinowski says:

> We start looking at how much capacity we have from the US to London in all classes of service. What we hope is that there is a correlation between the percentage of seats we have for a given route and the percentage of bookings we receive on that route. For example, if we hold 40 per cent of the seats to London, our goal is to have a minimum of 40 per cent of the bookings to London.

How does British Airways gather its data? When a travel agent makes a reservation, it uses a system known as CRS (Computer Reservation System). Five companies provide CRS terminals to agencies around the world. When making a reservation for a passenger, an agent collects a lot of information – origin, destination, seat, method of payment, home address, business address, food preferences, etc. This information is fed into a complex system that ensures, among other things, that travellers arrive at the correct destination, and that airlines receive payment for the seats.

Any airline can purchase this information from one of the CRS companies. British Airways spends millions of dollars a year buying that data for use world-wide, and Kalinowski makes sure it's put to good use:

> From this information, we are able to see things like what the market share is and what we are getting from the travel agency

community. From that, we can try to understand why, for example, we received 40 per cent of the bookings in business class to London for a given time period.

British Airways has refined the process even further. It looks not only at the average for the whole industry, but also at the data for small, individual travel agencies, various groups of agencies, and the mega-agencies like American Express or Rosenbluth International. It doesn't stop there. Kalinowski and the company explore the data down to its finest detail, down to cabin and city level, to reveal the most telling indicators.

The company then organizes this data into information and extrapolates knowledge that makes it possible for British Airways USA to say to the travel agency community: 'We will pay you for performance. We will pay you for giving us *more than* our natural share.' Kalinowski says:

> What British Airways USA has done is tell the travel agency community that we will pay a fair distribution fee to those who only distribute tickets, but we will pay a high sales commission to those who truly go out and promote and sell British Airways. We've made a distinction between someone who is *selling* a ticket and someone who is only *distributing* a ticket. If someone calls and says, 'I want to go to London,' you can promote the British Airways product. If you do that, we're going to reward you. Now you're a commissioned sales agent, just like any other commissioned sales agent for any product.

It took a great deal of work to reach the point where British Airways USA could implement its revolutionary plan. The company built up a massive database – one of the largest in the world – but raw data is of little use until someone takes it and turns it into information and acts on the learned knowledge.

Conclusion

With the increasing numbers of publications, books and magazines, and improvements in telecommunications, we need to learn how to read faster and remember more. We must be able to organize and structure information, and to turn information into knowledge. This is the process that will lead to creative breakthroughs.

ACTIVITIES

1. Solicit feedback from three customers who believe you have added value to their business. Document and review.

2. Open a 'Customer Knowledge' file. Collect relevant customer data and add this information to the file. Every month review the information. A good way to record and remember the data is to Mind Map the information and update the Mind Map monthly.

3. To develop your business brain, select a business topic of interest. Search for relevant books and sources of information on the subject and condense it all in one Mind Map.

4. Write a paper or newsletter on your area of expertise.

5. Choose a work topic where you are considered a subject expert and make a presentation to another department within your company.

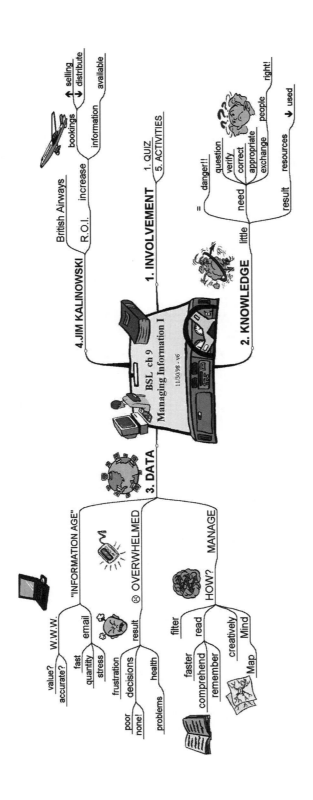

10 MANAGING INFORMATION II

Quiz

1. Do you have more reading than you are able to read?   Yes/No

2. Do you believe that your reading speed can be doubled?   Yes/No

3. Do you make linear notes when you are in a meeting or seminar?   Yes/No

4. Do you use graphics or pictures to support the message you are presenting in your business meetings?   Yes/No

5. Do you have problems remembering all the information required for your work?   Yes/No

6. Do you use colour in your note taking?   Yes/No

7. Do you use all your senses to improve your memory?   Yes/No

8. Have you been taught how to improve your memory?   Yes/No

9. Do you believe that taking frequent breaks helps improve your recall of new information?   Yes/No

10. Do you believe that your recall of information can exceed 90 per cent?   Yes/No

SCORING

Score two points for 'Yes' to all questions, except questions 1, 3 and 5 which score two points for 'No'.

If you scored over 18 points, congratulations! This chapter will help you fine-tune your reading and memory skills. If you scored 18 or less, this next chapter will show you how to strengthen your ability to input, store and recall information.

Overview

In this chapter, we will take a detailed look at some mental tools, including new approaches to reading and memory, and we'll examine how some companies and individuals have used them – with impressive results.

Coping with information

We live in an age of globalization, and information is being spread throughout the world at an ever increasing pace. The companies that survive and prosper will be those that have learned to harness that information and convert it into knowledge by developing the potential of the brains of their workforce. The growing recognition of this is reflected by the fact that many consultancy firms now have Chief Knowledge Officers or Learning Officers, and at least one university has appointed its first Professor of Knowledge.

To harness the power of learning, we need to install processes that increase creativity and generate breakthrough thinking. We must then spread that knowledge throughout our companies, so that individual departments don't have to reinvent the wheel.

READING FOR FUN AND PROFIT

Since a very high percentage of information is presented in the form of material that must be read, either on paper or, increasingly, on a computer screen, the single most important thing we can do to improve how we use information is to learn how to read faster and more efficiently. The first step in achieving this is to rethink how we learn new information.

The best approach is to skim through new material first, looking for any information you already know and understand. This allows your brain to identify a foundation of existing knowledge upon which to build new information.

If you are given a 30-page instruction booklet outlining the policies and procedures for a new job, the first thing to do is skim through the booklet, reading the headings and looking at any graphs and pictures. This serves two purposes: it gives you an idea of the overall flavour of the booklet, and it helps you draw up a mental map of what information is already familiar to you and what information is new.

In previous chapters, we discussed the importance of having a goal when approaching a task. This also applies to reading and learning new material. If you don't have a clear idea of what you need to learn, you will find it difficult to tell whether you have learned it, so it is helpful to read the conclusion of any new material before studying it in detail.

Next, begin a detailed study of the material, starting with the sections you understand completely, then moving on to the sections you have some familiarity with, and ending with the sections you know least about. This might mean that instead of reading the booklet from cover to cover, you read pages 4, 17, 23, 30, 1–3, 25–9, etc.

While this may appear to be a haphazard approach, it is the most efficient way to read the booklet, because it takes advantage of the way your brain works when absorbing new material – by linking it to ideas, concepts and facts it already knows.

Although most of us have been taught that a straightforward, linear approach to reading and studying is best, this is incorrect – and when it comes to reading, we tend to embrace many brain-unfriendly processes. *The Speed Reading Book* by Tony Buzan provides a list of 20 statements about reading. Many of the statements mentioned are what we were probably taught in school: for example, 'for better comprehension you should read slowly and carefully.' 'You should endeavour to understand 100 per cent of what you read.' 'Reading with your finger on the page slows you down, and should be eliminated with training.' These statements are wrong!

Reading more slowly does *not* increase comprehension, striving for 100 per cent comprehension is self-defeating, and placing a finger on the page does help the eyes move smoothly and naturally over the text.

Today, many people do much of their reading from a computer screen. This can lead to physical problems, from eyestrain to back pain. Some of the techniques to increase speed and efficiency in reading paper-based materials can be adapted to reading material on a VDU:

- Use a long, thin guide – a chopstick or knitting needle is ideal – as a substitute 'finger'. It allows your eye to track smoothly over the screen, and you can sit relaxed further away from the screen.
- Change the typeface displayed on the screen if the computer program allows you to do so. Experiment to find one that causes the least eyestrain.

- Take brief breaks every 15 to 20 minutes, resting your eyes by looking at objects in the far and middle distance range.

You need not be overwhelmed by the glut of information you must read and absorb. There is hope, and there is help. We have examined only some of the available techniques here. Further information on improving your reading speed and comprehension can be found in Buzan's *The Speed Reading Book.*

Oh, by the way, the one statement in the 20 assumptions about reading in Buzan's book that is correct is 'Reading speeds of more than 1 000 words per minute are possible.'

CONNECTING TO A BETTER MEMORY

These techniques for increasing your reading speed and efficiency will help you to deal more effectively with the vast quantities of information to which you are exposed every day, but how can you possibly remember it all? How can you recall it when you need it?

A recurrent theme in this book has been the way the brain links, connects and associates information. Anything you do to strengthen those links will improve your memory.

This means that you should pay attention to how you input the information into your memory in the first place.

Studies have demonstrated that if you use at least three of the five senses when learning new information, your recall of that material will exceed 90 per cent, so if you want to remember something, you should involve as many of your senses as possible.

Let's say that you need to memorize a set of figures for a presentation. When you look at the figures, you are using the first sense – vision. You can then write them down on a piece of paper, thus adding a second sense – touch. Your ability to recall those figures later will be greatly enhanced if you add at least one more sense. Perhaps you can read them aloud to yourself, ask someone to read the figures to you, or record them and play back the tape, so adding a third sense – hearing.

Each of the senses makes a different set of links, connections and associations, greatly increasing your ability to recall the figures later.

In addition to our five senses, we have ten cortical skills, as explained in

Chapter 4. These cortical skills are of immense value in memory. The more of them you can engage, the more links, connections and associations you will create in your brain.

Mind Maps harness these cortical skills, so they can be used to enhance memory and recall.

When people attempt to commit new information to memory, they use a variety of techniques: they may jot notes in the margins of the paper or book, highlight important passages, or make detailed, linear notes in a separate notebook. The first two methods work well, since they help clarify associations, but making linear notes as you read or study is the least successful, because it fails to do this. Mind Maps, on the other hand, draw on the brain's natural ability to link concepts, so they can not only help us absorb information, but also remember it, so that we can use it.

Mind Maps

Jim Deiner, a project manager for a Fortune 500 pharmaceutical company, recently had to prepare for a gruelling all-day certification test set by the Project Management Institute (PMI). The difficulty in preparing for this is that it tests the candidate's understanding of the entire field of project management, and this information can't be encapsulated in one comprehensive document, since it is the sum of the knowledge of all the practitioners and academics who apply and advance it. Deiner says: 'I used Mind Mapping as the vehicle to organize what I knew, and what I was learning, and to review a variety of different sources. It worked out very well.'

Deiner had to be proficient in eight knowledge areas. He prepared a separate Mind Map for each subject, using A3 sheets of paper.

He used the PMI book *A Guide to the Project Management Body of Knowledge* as a basic reference, and supplemented that with numerous other books. When he came across new information from any source, he added it to the Mind Map for the appropriate subject:

> As I worked go through any reference books I found, I would go back to the Mind Map and add the new material. I was integrating information from different sources, and they don't all organize it the same way. But with the Mind Maps, I could organize it consistently.

After his initial period of study, in which he integrated all the information he needed to learn into Mind Maps, Deiner was able to use them as a convenient and comprehensive revision aid:

> It was just eight pieces of paper. Some people use review books and flash cards. There is even some software, for $150, that basically quizzes you on things. Flash cards are OK, but they just carry one sentence per card. You ask yourself, 'What does this relate to?' But when you have it organized in a Mind Map, you can see the context; it has more meaning, and it stays with you more.

As exam time came nearer, Deiner used his Mind Maps for daily revision: 'I'd cover one sheet a day. First thing every day, over a cup of coffee, I would sit there and just read through it, and refresh myself.'

It became clear how valuable the Mind Maps had been when Deiner took the exam: 'Sometimes you couldn't tell what specific subject area they were testing. But in my mind it would pop up, and I could see the Mind Map, and read through it.'

Deiner passed the exam at his first attempt. Even now, he keeps his Mind Maps handy: 'I use them as a reference in my job. I've also used them in writing some project management reports.'

Timing and sequence

Memory is a complex phenomenon, and scientists are continuously making discoveries about how it works. Take the matter of timing or sequence. We usually remember the first thing we read in a session and the last thing we read before taking a break. We also remember any material in between that is unusual or remarkable, but we recall the rest less well. We call this tendency to remember the first and last items that are studied 'the primacy-recency effect'.

This suggests a useful approach when learning new information – take frequent breaks. If you add additional beginning and ending points, you increase the amount of material you are likely to remember, and decrease the period in which items are more likely to be forgotten.

Forty-five minutes is the maximum time you should spend in one sitting learning new material; half an hour is even better. At the end of each session, take a five-minute break to stretch and relax, giving your brain time to integrate what you have been learning.

The primacy-recency effect is an important point to remember when you are planning a training session or seminar. If you need to conduct two hours of training, rather than scheduling one two-hour session, break it up into four half-hour sessions. Unfortunately, this is not the norm. Too many seminars or training workshops are scheduled in two-hour sessions. The brain's natural memory rhythm runs in cycles of 30–50 minutes. Working with that natural rhythm enhances the ability to recall. Working against it makes recall much more difficult.

Remember the brain's natural rhythm when you call on a customer. A New York City salesman recently complained that he had given a customer literature and information, but when he went back to visit him one month later, the customer had forgotten everything that had been presented.

'The visit was made just 30 minutes before lunch. The customer had four things going on at once, and I was competing with everyone who was trying to catch him before he left to eat.' said the salesman.

To maximize the effectiveness of the customers' recall of your presentation, you need to be the last person he sees before lunch, or the first person he sees after lunch.

There is another brain rhythm that has a significant impact on memory: the pattern and frequency of your revision of the material. To maximize your ability to recall new information, you should review it one hour later, then again one day later, one week later, and finally, one month later. After this fourth review, the material will require only minimal revision in the future to keep it locked in your memory.

We are constantly learning new facts about our remarkable memories. Readers who wish to explore this further will find a wealth of information on techniques for enhancing memory in Tony Buzan's book, *Use Your Memory.*

APPLYING INFORMATION

We have discussed ways to store information in our brains more quickly and effectively, and we have discussed ways to improve our recall of that material. The next stage is to apply that information to create value for your company and clients. Among other things, that means distributing relevant information throughout your company so that every individual and every department can benefit by it. Marshall Tarley of ASCAP (American Society of Composers, Authors and Publishers) provides us with an excellent example of just how that can be done with the aid of Mind Maps.

Tarley, Director of Team Development for ASCAP's Broadcast Licensing Division, has used Mind Maps for note-taking, brainstorming, creating a group consensus, planning, and to communicate ideas to other departments in his organization.

'Success depends on good communication,' Tarley says, 'and words often aren't enough. Mind Mapping, with its use of multiple cortical skills such as colour, image, symbols and language, is an excellent communication tool.'

Tarley's team was asked to make a presentation to a task force that was reorganizing a division of the company. The task force posed a number of questions about the work Tarley's team was doing, and why it took so many people to do it:

> The business area that I manage is rather complex. It encompasses licensing, sales, customer service, collections and a lot of analysis and data processing. It wasn't going to be easy to demonstrate this to the task force quickly and clearly. We thought Mind Mapping would be the most effective way of presenting it.

> We created a Mind Map that was about six feet high and six feet wide. We started out with a central image of a musical signature, and used stick figures to represent members of the team, each in a different colour.

> The musical signature represented the music licence, the different-coloured stick figures represented the diversity of the functions of the team, the cultural diversity of the people on the team, and their different skill sets.

> Then we had TV sets popping out in a circle, because we license music to TV. They appeared like gears in a well-tooled machine.

The Mind Map included colour-coded branches for the various processes performed by the team, the systems that support each process, and their impacts on internal and external customers.

Tarley's team was unsure about how the presentation would be accepted by the members of the task force, none of whom were familiar with Mind Mapping:

> We gave a relatively brief presentation, with three of us taking turns. At the conclusion of our presentation, the task force was blown away. They said, 'Wow, you seem to be doing the kinds of things on your team that we want for the whole division . . . We never realized what you do and how much you do.' As a result, the task force adopted our organizational structure for the whole division.

Now *that*'s effective communication.

Leadership profile: Rosenbluth International

KNOWLEDGE AND INFORMATION

If any company in the USA is plagued with a never-ending torrent of information, it's Rosenbluth International, which specializes in corporate travel. Air fares, car rental rates and hotel room charges vary on a daily basis, and there are thousands of changes from each supplier which affect how much clients will have to pay, as well as Rosenbluth's profits.

Supplier information isn't the only information it has to manage, either. Rosenbluth International must also know a great deal about its clients, such as what their time and budget constraints are and what individuals expect of their travel arrangements. Capturing this information and turning it into useful knowledge has become a science at Rosenbluth International. Since 1994, the staff have been refining a proprietary computer program called DACODA (Discount Analysis Containing Optimal Decision Algorithms), which takes massive amounts of complicated information and distils it to decide on the best purchasing strategy for clients. Not only do the agents then have access to up-to-date fare knowledge via their computers, they can also call up each customer's profile to see what their needs and requirements are, enabling them to make the right match.

'This system allows customers to make choices which give them the most for their money,' said Mike McCormick, Vice-president of Supplier Relations for Rosenbluth International. 'Before, we were limited to what you could do with a spreadsheet and some smart people. With this innovative technology, we can now help companies spend their travel budget intelligently, so they get greater value.'

Most of the data-processing is automated. Based on a model designed by Rosenbluth personnel in Mike's department which screens out what isn't pertinent, information flows in electronically from a variety of sources.

Mike's staff are constantly evaluating this information and making adjustments as necessary, to create a system that is as comprehensive as possible. 'We try to make the net broad,' said Mike. 'We don't want to limit our view and only pay attention to a few areas.' The company places heavy emphasis on studying the travel industry, rather than relying on outside experts.

'We have many specialists in the company,' said Hal Rosenbluth, President and CEO. 'With our customers in mind, we study suppliers in the kind of depth that a Wall Street firm would study the stock market for their investors. We find out everything there is to know about each airline, each hotel chain, each car rental firm. We get to know its behaviour, corporate culture, direction and goals. We have one person devoted to studying each company. I trust these individuals to sift out the appropriate information.'

Rosenbluth International has become a news service for the travel industry, with publications which feature both trends in the travel business and daily updates on changes. Their products are called *MarketPLACE* and *MarketWATCH*. *MarketPLACE* is an update on the travel industry in areas that are of key importance to Rosenbluth customers, and is sent to customers and agents via e-mail. *MarketWATCH* is published monthly, carrying trend information about such matters as fares. The collection and distribution of the information is automated, and is overseen by an editor. 'The combination of these technologies and our associates is powerful,' said Mike. 'This is what sets us apart from other travel companies.'

When gathering information that you hope to turn into knowledge, Mike advises that you follow one simple rule: go to the original source of any information you intend to use. 'It's no good basing decisions on other people's summaries,' he says. 'Information from a third party might be inaccurate or incomplete. We go right to the source.'

Conclusion

In this chapter, we examined just a few examples of people who have learned to tap into the natural power of the brain, and in doing so have made an enormous difference in their organizations. We can all learn to do this. We can all learn to tap into the tremendous capacity of the human brain, and unleash a firestorm of creativity and innovation.

ACTIVITIES

1. **Conduct meetings that include all current employees who deal with specific business processes. Have each team member share critical details of their work.**

2. **Quarterly meetings can be powerful communication vehicles. Create a structure for them so that they are interesting, exciting, and carry specific learning objectives.**

3. **Mind Map the minutes of your next business meeting.**

4. **Take a course on speed reading, and measure your reading improvement over the next six months.**

5. **Attend a seminar on improving your memory, and use the skills you learn to improve your work procedures.**

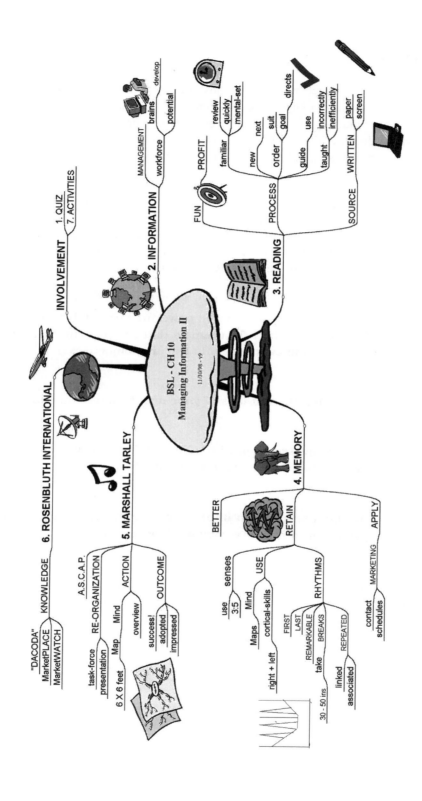

INVOLVEMENT
1. QUIZ
7. ACTIVITIES

2. INFORMATION
MANAGEMENT
workforce — brains — develop
potential

3. READING
FUN
PROFIT
new — familiar — review — quickly — mental-set
order — next — suit — goal — directs
PROCESS
guide — use
taught — incorrectly — inefficiently
SOURCE
WRITTEN
paper
screen

BSL - CH 10
Managing Information II
11/30/98 - v9

4. MEMORY
BETTER
RETAIN
use
senses
3:5
Maps
Mind
right + left — cortical-skills
FIRST
LAST
REMARKABLE
RHYTHMS
take — BREAKS — REPEATED
linked
associated
30 - 50 ins
USE
contact
schedules
MARKETING
APPLY

6. ROSENBLUTH INTERNATIONAL
"DACODA"
MarketPLACE
KNOWLEDGE
MarketWATCH

5. MARSHALL TARLEY
A.S.C.A.P.
task-force
presentation
RE-ORGANIZATION
6 X 6 feet
Map
Mind
ACTION
overview
success!
adopted
impressed
OUTCOME

11 PROCESS INNOVATION THROUGH TEAMS

Quiz

1. Do you maintain a list or Mind Map of activities that you currently perform on a daily or weekly basis?   Yes/No

2. Do you have a method for assessing the value of these activities to the company?   Yes/No

3. Do you have a method of measuring your performance for these activities?   Yes/No

4. If you do your job well, is it unnecessary to understand the final use to which your work is put?   Yes/No

5. Do you have a way of prioritizing which of your activities you should improve?   Yes/No

6. Do you know who the key people are who would influence the way any of these activities are performed?   Yes/No

7. Do you know who your allies and non-supporters are in this improvement process?   Yes/No

8. Have you compared your performance for each activity against someone else who also performs the same activity?   Yes/No

9. Do you have an ongoing process to update your customer requirements?   Yes/No

10. If customers don't complain, can you assume that all is well?   Yes/No

SCORING

Score two points for each question that was answered 'Yes,' except questions 4 and 10 which score two points for 'No'.

If you scored 18 points or more, you have an excellent understanding of the subject and this chapter will help you refine your skill. If you scored less than 18 points, this chapter will add significantly to your leadership development.

Overview

Having examined many of the latest advances in our understanding of how the brain works, and how that understanding can help us be more efficient and effective in our daily lives, this chapter will show you how all that information has been integrated into a comprehensive programme that helps businesses achieve remarkable results. This is the method behind Rich Bannon's success story (see Chapter 1).

Imagine that one morning, your manager pays you an unexpected visit. He or she offers to help you fix the most important business problem you presently face. You pick the most annoying, frustrating problem that comes up every month, and eats up hours and hours of your time in tedious, mind-numbing work.

Your manager laughs and says, 'Consider it done!' A cloud of smoke clears, and you are surrounded by familiar faces. You had not been aware that the same problem that drives you to distraction is also plaguing five other people elsewhere in your company.

Your manager holds a group discussion using a business language that leads the six of you to speak and listen to each other in a new way, as if walls and barriers were suddenly taken away. As the meeting imparts each new piece of knowledge to you, your mind creates new links and associations about how this process can be applied to so many other pressing business problems, and seemingly in the same instant, you think of so many ways you can use these same tools to improve your life and the lives of those around you.

By the time the meeting ends, you and your associates have a defined, achievable goal, a timetable, a plan, and the tools to achieve it. Your group, with its new-found cameraderie and enthusiasm, knows that this is just the beginning, and you know that a door has opened – those issues you once viewed as problems, you now see as opportunities. You have the power to communicate with each other, understand the whole picture, and the power to create solutions that benefit your customers and your company. You also recognize you add value to your company.

Does this seem like a fantasy? The fact is, using the Process Innovation Through Teams (PITT) workshop, it has happened many times.

One of the key features of the PITT workshop is that it uses participants' own work situations as the vehicle for applying new skills and creating change. Employees who attend the workshop become creative assets for their company, able to size up business issues and look for the opportunities to make continuous innovation the standard.

Another benefit of the workshops is a reduction of the 25–30 per cent of employees' time spent in making adjustments and correcting errors. We will discuss this later in the chapter.

The importance of teamwork

We learned in Chapter 6 about the advantages of applying the TEFCAS model to our work. We will now apply this approach to the work of the company as a whole, and to the processes that are involved.

You will remember that TEFCAS is an approach to working at maximum efficiency, and TEFCAS stands for Try-all, Event, Feedback, Check, Adjust and Success. We started our discussion of TEFCAS with the final letter, 'S', which stands for Success in achieving a goal.

Here we'll let that 'S' represent the end product or service that will be provided to the customer. If we look at it that way, it's immediately clear that for the whole process to work most efficiently, every employee should know what the customer's requirements are – *every* employee, from trainees to top executives.

In too many companies, however, most employees have only a vague idea of how their work really fits into the big picture, and as a result, much of the work that they do is misdirected and generally inefficient.

Since the brain craves completeness, it will strive to fill in any blanks with assumptions, as we learned in Chapter 3. Those assumptions can be very far off the mark. If you hear people saying things like 'I thought . . .', 'I believe . . .', 'I assume . . .', you know that they are just filling in the blanks. If they really knew, really understood, they would be saying, 'I know . . .'. If they did know, they would be able to add detail to enrich the picture, as happens in teams working with Mind Maps.

CASE STUDY

Vincent Liuzza Jr

The details that enrich the picture of a successful outcome can come from any employee, as the owner of a restaurant in Louisiana discovered. Vincent Liuzza Jr, President of CuCo's Mexican Restaurants, used Mind Maps to solve a difficult problem he was facing. A high crime rate in the neighbourhood surrounding the restaurant was keeping diners away. Vince designed a master Mind Map that was made available to all members of the staff, from the maître d' to the assistant waiters. It allowed everyone to see the big picture (the high crime rate, and its impact on restaurant business), and to contribute their ideas for solving the problem.

One of the waiters proposed that staff should walk the customers back to their cars as they left the restaurant, to give them a feeling of security. His proposal was implemented, the number of customers soared, and business boomed.

Efficient Processes Require a Clear Picture of Success.

The output of a company is in some ways like a giant jigsaw puzzle that is being put together for the benefit of a customer, with each employee contributing a number of pieces of the puzzle (we use 'customer' here to refer to not only the external final customer, but also the internal user of the output of any process at any stage).

Quite often, employees work with their individual pieces without ever knowing what the completed puzzle will look like. This is a common cause of inefficient processes. What are the results? Workers and managers are preoccupied with overcoming crises created by an absence of communication and a lack of skill in focusing on the root causes of problems and creating solutions. The whole process works best when every employee knows exactly how their pieces of work link to the adjacent pieces, and to the puzzle as a whole.

Once workers and managers improve their communication, everyone can understand the whole process. This teamwork develops into an extraordinary power, creating solutions that improve the functioning of the company and everyone within it.

Team members should be taught how to define the output requirements of their activities, and how they relate to the whole process. Mind Maps can be used very effectively in process analysis. Clarifying customer requirements leads to an automatic improvement in work, because of the brain's success-driven mechanism, and the relationships between different activities and tasks are revealed.

In the words of Rich Bannon: 'If you take any process and break it down into its component pieces, you will have a tool box under your arm that you can use to solve any business process problem you will ever encounter.'

Process analysis

In analysing work processes, people tend to become confused because they do not understand the differences between a *process*, a *subprocess*, an *activity* and a *task*. People often use these terms as though they were interchangeable. They are not.

TASKS

Tasks are the detailed steps that a person performs in transforming input into output. A task is the lowest level of a person's work action or behaviour that can be studied, quantified or analysed. The tasks for a clerk who sets up appointments for the sales staff, for example, might include phoning a prospect, making an appointment, and entering the appointment date and time on a master schedule.

ACTIVITIES

Related tasks are grouped into an activity (see Figure 11.1). An activity will normally include 15–20 tasks.

Each employee performs several activities as part of their day-to-day job. Each activity involves transforming something that they receive from another employee or department (input), and passing it on to someone else (output) – this could be anything from adding parts on an assembly line to entering information into a database. A white-collar worker, for example, frequently receives information from other functions (suppliers), and performs a series of tasks to convert the data into a meaningful analysis. The analysis (output) is then sent to an internal customer, who might use it to prepare a monthly financial report. Examples

What is an Activity?

Activity Defined:

'A Series of Tasks Which Transform An Input Into An Output.'

(Tasks)

Figure 11.1 Definition of an activity

of activities for a salesperson could include identifying and meeting with new clients, informing existing customers of a new product offering, or creating a monthly report that summarizes client contacts and is reviewed by the vice president of sales.

SUBPROCESSES

A subprocess is a grouping of several related activities that are part of a bigger process.

PROCESSES

Activities and sub-processes are linked together to form a process. A process involves linking or sequencing activities in an orderly fashion with the aim of creating some specified output for a defined set of customers (see Figure 11.2). Linking and sequencing are among the cortical skills of the human brain that we discussed in Chapter 4.

There may be 30 or 40 processes going on at the same time in any company, usually performed by many different departments and people (see Figure 11.3).

Link Work Activities into a Process Flow to Achieve Maximum Results

A process is defined as the organization of people, procedures, machines and materials into work activities needed to produce a specified end result.

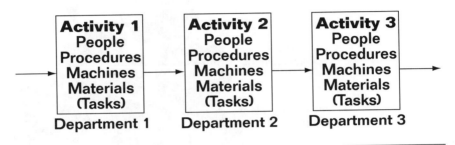

Figure 11.2 Process definition chart

The relationship between work and organizational structure

The organizational structure of nearly all companies involves three levels:

1. **Workers doing their daily jobs** – This is where tasks and activities are accomplished. At this level, there is often little understanding of the processes that exist within the company, or how individuals' activities fit into them.
2. **Middle management** – Middle managers typically view work from the perspective of activities and subprocesses. Since middle managers are responsible for co-ordinating higher-level (process) views of work with lower-level (task) knowledge, to be successful they must understand tasks, activities and processes.
3. **Senior management** – Top executives understand work at the process level, frequently having little or no knowledge of either activities or tasks.

All three levels must work together if the company is to be successful. Far too often, however, they don't, leading to customer dissatisfaction and inefficiency.

> # Much like the gears of a smooth-running machine, a process has a series of tight-fitting, interconnected parts.

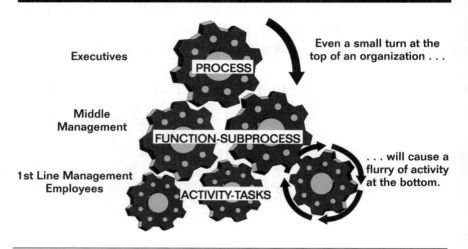

Executives

Even a small turn at the top of an organization . . .

Middle Management

FUNCTION-SUBPROCESS

1st Line Management Employees

ACTIVITY-TASKS

. . . will cause a flurry of activity at the bottom.

Figure 11.3 Gear chart

Problems with Communication of Work Can Have Disastrous Results

In an effective organization, all three levels communicate using the same terms, and make the same links and connections to the defined goals. When this occurs, company-wide agreement exists on how to prioritize the company's resources in alignment with the goals.

EXECUTIVE (PROCESS) LEVEL

At the top level of the company, executives have a responsibility to set goals, direction and strategies – such as growing market share, increasing profits, maintaining happy customers – and then deciding what processes must be performed and what resources must be made available to achieve them. They must see the big picture, the complete puzzle.

However, executives frequently don't know what work is performed at the lower levels, and how their decisions affect those workers. They must ensure that relevant information and knowledge is shared between all the appropriate people at all levels of the organization, so that more intelligent decisions can be made, taking into account the impact of those decisions.

MIDDLE MANAGER (ACTIVITY/SUBPROCESS) LEVEL

Between the executives and staff are the middle managers, who sometimes have the most difficult job of all. They must interpret the decisions of the executives, translate them into activities and tasks, communicate them to the workers, and then see that they are carried out.

Interpretation can lead to pitfalls. In one company, the president and a vice president were talking in the cafeteria. The president expressed curiosity about maintenance figures in some of their service contracts. The vice president returned to his office and ordered a complete analysis of maintenance costs for the company's product line. When the report was sent to the president, he asked the vice president what it was all about. When the vice president said he had ordered it as a result of their conversation, the surprised president said that he had only been making idle conversation, not expecting a report that took up two weeks' work.

STAFF (TASK/ACTIVITY) LEVEL

At the staff level, employees often don't know how their work fits into the process. They don't know how it relates to the next person in the link. They don't know exactly what the consequences will be if their work contains errors, fails to be completed on time, or isn't it completed at all, and they don't know what the overall goals and strategies of the company are – they don't know what the completed puzzle, the big picture, should look like. It's not that they don't care: in most cases, they simply don't have the time, because they are too busy performing tasks to ask questions about matters that don't seem relevant to their work. Unless an education programme is instigated to impart this knowledge, it can sometimes only be gained through years of experience in the company.

Companies that downsize often lose the experience of older workers. New employees have to spend a lot of time trying to learn about their pieces of the puzzle, so that they can appreciate what they contribute to the process, often resulting in painful lessons, a greater unit cost per output, and a lower level of service than would occur in an organization where workers had a good understanding of the relationship between tasks, activities and processes.

One company suffered severe penalties because a new employee didn't realize the importance of a particular piece of paper he handled. The employee took a printout from a computer and threw it on top of a pile of papers, then left for the day. The printout was the quarterly financial forecast that the president of the company was expecting to be on his desk the next morning. When it didn't arrive, the embarrassed president was unable to tell a number of Wall Street analysts the latest quarterly earnings. As this illustrates, a failure of communication can mean anything from a minor annoyance (in the case of the unwanted maintenance report) to utter disaster (failing to send financial results to the company president).

The Process Innovation Through Teams Workshop Helps Bridge the Communication Gap.

The PITT workshop helps companies bridge the communications gap. It teaches staff how to explain their job activities clearly, and it also helps them to define any problems they are experiencing in performing their work. In this way, they can see the bigger picture (see Figure 11.4).

The PITT programme makes use of the Brain Principles we have talked about earlier in this book, and the fact that the brain likes to think in pictures and visual images, as discussed in Chapter 4.

According to this theory, when talking with someone who isn't familiar with an employee's job or day-to-day activities, the employee should use words that paint a picture of the tasks involved in the mind of the listener. The employee should use an action verb and a noun, and make the description both specific and observable.

One department's output is another department's input.

We are all connected to the bigger picture

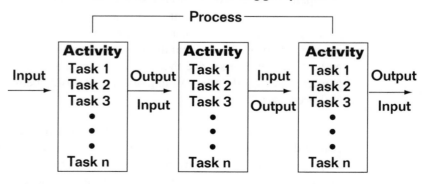

Figure 11.4 The bigger picture

BrainSmart!

A creative process would involve:

- Mind Mapping a definition of the problem and the goal (see Chapter 4)
- generating ideas from all relevant staff as to why the problem exists and how to solve it (see Chapters 3 and 4)
- exchanging these ideas (see Chapter 10)
- creating group solutions (see Chapter 4)
- evaluating the solutions
- planning steps of action
- evaluating the process (see Chapter 6, TEFCAS in action).

Employees' ability to paint word-pictures of their job activities paves the way for a review process that can help a company understand and measure it. This allows new links and associations to develop, leading to creative solutions to process problems.

So how do we take this thinking and use it to address the organizational issues of the business, and how do we synthesize and bring together the diversity of opinion on a team?

Performing an Activity Analysis

STEP 1: CREATE AN ACTIVITY LIST

The first step in performing an Activity Analysis is to list all the work activities you perform as part of your job. The activity description should be as detailed as possible, and include both a noun and an action verb. A well-described activity would allow an unfamiliar listener to form a clear mental picture of the work being performed.

After creating a list of activities, the next step is to add some evaluative elements to each activity:

1. Estimate the potential for improvement, especially by improving those activities which lead to errors or rework.
2. Gauge the effort needed to achieve the improvement: high, medium or low. For example, 'high' could mean six people working full-time for six months; 'medium' might mean three people working part-time

BrainSmart!

Tips for activity list:

- The activity list should represent what is currently being done, not what should be done in an ideal situation.
- When prioritizing your list for the purpose of making a change or improvement, ensure that the opportunity for improvement can be clearly articulated for each activity.

for three months, 'low' might mean two people working two hours a week for two months.

3. Identify whose approval you will need to make changes to the activity or tasks.
4. Estimate the time that will elapse before the actions produce benefits.

STEP 2: TASK ANALYSIS

The next step in the Activity Analysis process is to select an activity for task analysis. An ideal activity is one which has great potential for improvement, requires a small amount of time to achieve improvement, has a favourable approval authority, and which will take a short time to realize the benefits.

Performing a disciplined task analysis of current work allows the brain to see work as it is actually performed. From this the brain can then begin to question why these steps are being performed in this sequence and in this manner, and may generate blanks which lead it to create new sequencing.

A detailed task analysis helps break workers out of 'robot mode', where they are doing things by rote simply because that is the way they have always done them.

Step 2.1: Categorizing and Prioritizing Tasks
After listing all the tasks performed in the activity, the next step is to prioritize them based upon their importance, effort and nature. In evaluating the nature of tasks (why they are performed), we define them as falling into one of four categories:

- Required
- Failure

BrainSmart!

Tips for task description:

- The detailed list should be drawn up in sequence to match the way the work is actually being performed.
- Ensure that all rework and corrective steps which are current tasks are included.

- Appraisal
- Preventive.

Required tasks are those that are essential. Even if we lived in a perfect world in which nobody ever made any mistakes, these tasks would be necessary in order to transform an input into an output. An example of this would be filing paperwork with a government agency to ensure compliance with regulations.

Failure tasks are undertaken when something has gone wrong or a mistake has been made, resulting in the need for remedial action. With so much pressure on companies to reduce costs, this provides an opportunity to eliminate expense, and at the same time improve efficiency. Experience with the PITT programme has shown that 25–30 per cent of staff time at the task level is spent doing something connected with adjusting, correcting, reworking or writing off work already done.

The most common reason for a failure task is an unclear or incorrect definition of a customer requirement. If the supplier of your information does not know the best format for you to receive input, you may receive input that requires substantial rework on your part. If you do not have a clear definition of what *your* customer needs, you may be inadvertently supplying them with output that will need to be reworked or written off. One example would be a new procedure that is put in place without clearly understanding the requirements of all the people who will have to implement it.

Appraisal tasks occur whenever there is a suspicion that mistakes are being made, or that output is not reliable enough to be sent without checking it first. An appraisal task involves inspecting or checking an output to sort good from bad. For example, if we type a letter, somebody must proofread it before we send it, or when somebody produces a financial report, before it is circulated somebody must check all the numbers

BrainSmart!

More than a quarter of work done by employees involves correcting or adjusting for errors. Clearly, reducing that wasted effort can reap great rewards for a company. If companies facing a downsizing were to focus on the 25–30 per cent of effort wasted correcting mistakes instead of making arbitrary staff cuts, they would be able to make dramatic improvements in their service to their customers. Clearly a win-win situation.

against the accounting ledger. On average, 5–10 per cent of a company's costs are connected to appraisal tasks.

Preventive tasks are pre-emptive actions taken before an output has been created with the conscious aim of trying to avoid or prevent an error from being made in the first place.

It is clear that devoting resources to preventive tasks will be more efficient and cost-effective than correcting mistakes after they have been made. (See Figure 11.5) It's not enough to find and correct errors. It is more important to look for the root source of errors, and make adjustments in our tasks and activities to prevent similar errors from happening in the future.

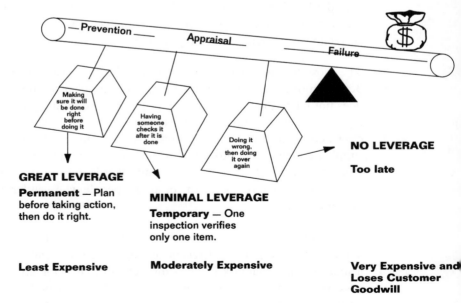

Figure 11.5 Comparison of leverage for three types of task

BrainSmart!

Tips for categorizing tasks:

- Normally, in the sequence of how tasks are performed a failure task will follow an appraisal.
- Prevention tasks maximize leverage to reduce failures.

Unfortunately, our experience indicates that very often *no* time is spent on preventive tasks – we are too busy fixing yesterday's problems. As we learned in Chapter 3, the brain has an infinite capacity for generating new ideas. We must learn to put that ability to work on finding ways to prevent problems, rather than wasting effort finding ways to correct problems after they have occurred.

This is not to imply that investing time in preventive tasks will be easy. In fact, you will temporarily *increase* your workload, since you will be correcting errors at the same time as adding steps to ensure that the errors won't happen again. Because of that increased workload, the natural tendency is to concentrate on the fixes and neglect the preventive measures. If preventive actions don't lead to immediate improvements people often give up before the root causes of the failures are eliminated, and go back to living with the problems. Therefore, how people prioritize their activity list is critical to their long-term success.

The goal of task analysis is to identify the tasks that offer the least added value to the activity in question. The best method for improving the efficiency of an activity is to minimize appraisal tasks and eliminate failure tasks. The use of Mind Maps is an excellent way to generate ideas at this stage.

STEP 3: MEETING WITH CUSTOMERS AND SUPPLIERS

The next step in Activity Analysis is to obtain feedback on your activity and task list (the 'F' in TEFCAS – see Chapter 6). This may come from a manager or supervisor, the next person in the link, the previous person in the link (the supplier), or the person who receives the output from the worker (the customer). Feedback can also be obtained at a meeting in which several workers exchange ideas. You must decide what you will measure through this feedback, so that you can take appropriate action (see Figure 11.6).

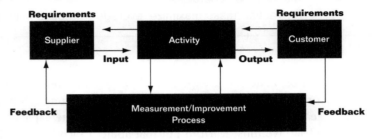

What will you measure, and how will you use it?

Measurement means comparing output to user requirements

Figure 11.6 Input/output feedback chart

The feedback will consider a number of factors involved in the process, including the cost to the company of implementing any solution, how long it would take to improve matters, and who in the company would need to approve any changes.

Meeting with your customers and suppliers to draw up a clear definition of requirements is the best way to eliminate failure tasks.

THE PROCESS INNOVATION THROUGH TEAMS WORKSHOP

The most effective way to introduce a PITT Workshop is to group 20 to 25 employees into four or five work-related teams. The workshop uses Activity Analysis and Mind Mapping to create process innovation breakthroughs.

Activity Analysis begins when the team of participants creates a list of work activities that are part of a process. Team members then pick one of the activities for detailed analysis to identify areas of possible improvement. Participants are encouraged to start small – find an activity that can be immediately improved. As team members increase in confidence based on their initial success, they can look for additional avenues for improvement. Figure 11.7 shows an example of an activity list from an IBM payroll department team.

Problems at the task-specific level are all too frequently compounded because of the failure to translate them into broader-based process management issues. This ultimately creates communications gaps, poor

BrainSmart!

Tip for customer/supplier:

- When discussing requirements with your customer or supplier, be open – it may lead to product innovations.

employee morale, inefficiency and additional process costs due to unnecessary spending. To help teams bridge this communication gap, PITT Workshops demonstrate how to use Mind Maps to organize thinking, structure the problem-solving process, and improve communication in the brain blooming process.

Each team must agree on a key problem they are going to solve. This is reflected by the central image of a Mind Map. In the brain blooming process, each team member creates their own central image of the problem which needs to be solved, then the team combines these images into a central image. When a team cannot agree on a central image, this provides an early warning that they will not be successful in producing meaningful results. It is revealing to compare the different perspectives that surface when team members compare their drawings.

The communication that takes place while creating the central image for the Mind Map is powerful, and this common focal point is essential to generate creative solutions, and to build the team consensus necessary to implement them.

The main branches radiating from the central image in Figure 11.8 are created for each of the elements of the definition of a process – people, procedures, machinery and materials. The branches are not added sequentially, but are completed randomly by team members as their search for the cause of the problem triggers ideas.

Mind Mapping gives a team a clear vision of their goals. It forces them to consider the entire problem by showing them an overall picture of it. Once the team has agreed on a central image, the various branches help them organize their thoughts in a logical manner, and allow them to see the interdependence of all the elements.

The process of creating the central image shows the team how the individual members can look at a problem in a unique way, and each

Activity List

				✔ Noun	
				✔ Action Verb	
				✔ Specific	
PART OF WHICH PROCESS? Payroll				✔ Observable	
GENERAL DESCRIPTION OF YOUR WORK PERFORMED WITHIN YOUR DEPARTMENT OR PROCESS (LISTING MAJOR OR ALL ACTIVITIES)	Y/N	H/M/L	😊 😊 😞	1 month/ 3 months/ 1 year?	
Analysing payment problems for employees	Y	M	😊	3 months	
Handling customer escalations	Y	M	😊	3 months	
Handling customers regarding payroll issues	Y	M	😊	3 months	
Creating clerical cheques	Y	M	😊	1 month	
Auditing and signing clerical cheques	Y	M	😊	3 months	
Controlling clerical cheques	Y	M	😊	1 month	

Y/N? — Is there an opportunity for improvement or elimination of a failure task?
H/M/L? — What is the scale of the effort needed to fix the failure?
😊😊😞 — Is the approval authority a happy, neutral or hostile person in relation to this activity?
1 month (etc.)? — How long before successful results will be realized?

Figure 11.7   Example of an activity list

unique vision can be integrated into the whole. The insights gained from the Mind Map can help team members bridge communication gaps that exist between staff and executives. The pictures and branches make it easy for anyone unfamiliar with the day-to-day details to understand the whole problem and provide assistance.

Let's take a look at a PITT Workshop at IBM that successfully used Mind Maps and Activity Analysis to create team synergy. Note the central image 'Lotsa $' in Figure 11.8. It reflected the team's dismay when they started to realize the resources the company needed just to process clerical cheques. Their Activity Analysis had shown them that 90 minutes were spent each day handling cheques outside the normal process. The cost of $50 to correct one cheque multiplied by the 20 cheques handled each month resulted in a failure cost of $1 000 per month.

In one phase of the workshop, the Mind Map created by the team showed team members that they could achieve savings of 30 minutes per day simply by changing the *sequence* of tasks involved in performing the activity. The team did so, and advised their managers of the change in procedure. The number of clerical cheques was immediately reduced by 90 per cent and the team saved 30 hours' work each month, and $1 000.

Creative Process Ideas Come in Small Steps.

It is wise to remember that important advances do not usually occur through large, unexpected jumps, but result from the clarity with which the goal has been established and the amount of time spent developing creative ideas.

For this reason, to maximize team creativity, don't cut short the Mind Mapping brain-blooming session, either individually or in a group. The most common reason for failing to develop creative ideas is that the group switches too quickly from generating ideas to evaluating them. This may seem obvious, but it happens all the time.

The additional time and effort spent by an individual or a group beyond when they first believe they have finished developing new ideas greatly increases the probability that an unrelated outside stimulus will trigger an insight – an 'A-ha!'

Creative thinking is a repetitive process. The best way to increase creativity is to increase the number of small refinements that are made in each idea generated. This leads to increasingly innovative ideas.

At the beginning of a group attempt at finding solutions, the team must *decide* to be creative. Some people may have trouble with this concept – they don't understand how one can 'decide' to be creative. Too many people think that you are either creative, or you're not. But creativity is an act of will. If you decide to be creative, you will discover, perhaps to your surprise, that you become creative. Why is that true? Many people become less creative as they become more successful, because they are loath to challenge the status quo that has done well for them in the past. Their energy becomes focused on playing not to lose, rather than creating new ideas. Rather than working to generate new links and associations, they spend their time criticizing other ideas or explaining why 'that just won't work'.

Experience and memory play a critical role in the creative process. They

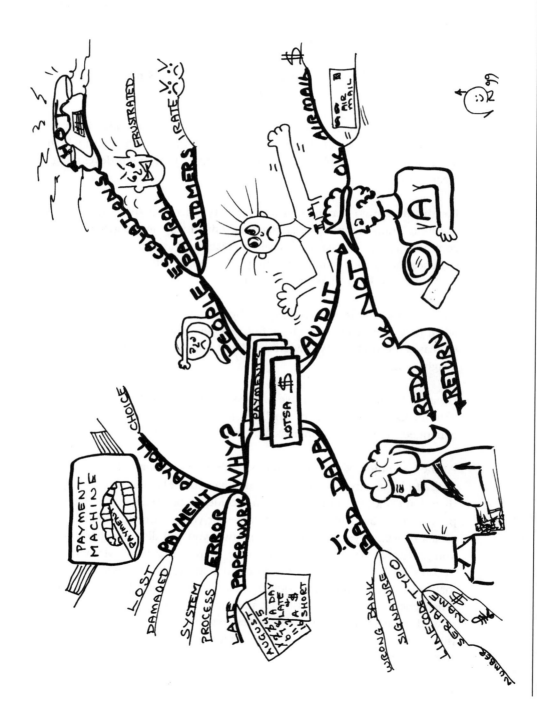

Figure 11.8 Clerical Cheques Mind Map

are the starting points to which new ideas are linked, associated and connected.

In a group environment, the combined experience of all the individuals present can exponentially increase the number of creative ideas brought forth, as discussed in Chapter 7. Ideally, a group will consist of both 'left-brain' people – those with strong analytical, logical, numerical and verbal skills – and 'right-brain' people – those who are imaginative, able to see the big picture, and have good visualization skills.

Sandy Hahn of IBM (see Chapter 7) recognized this when she put together a team that was charged with simplifying the international tax reconciliation process while also increasing customer satisfaction. Hahn identified the strongest cortical skills within each team member, and harnessed their diverse backgrounds to generate creativity and innovation.

At the completion of the project, Hahn's team exceeded all existing performance targets and attained all its goals – a zero backlog of tax reconciliations, 100 per cent attainment of settlements, and customer satisfaction of better than 90 per cent.

The rich diversity of experience and attitude can create a synergy which makes the group a fountain of creative ideas. If poorly managed, however, the diversity becomes divisive, with the group arguing over whose viewpoint is 'right'.

PITT success stories

IBM has been extremely successful at harnessing the energy and creativity that comes from team effort using Mind Maps and the other tools developed through our increased understanding of how the brain works.

ANDY GUERRIERI'S STORY

Andy Guerrieri used his understanding of process to solve a thorny problem involving payments to foreign brokers.

In the early 1990s, IBM experimented with changing the way it imported parts from IBM plants outside the USA. Previously, the company had used outside export brokers in the country in which the IBM plant was located, and import brokers in the USA. In 1994, however, the company decided to handle imports in-house.

The change had some unintended consequences. After several months, there was a developing debate between the local accounts payable department and the import operations department over the fact that foreign brokers weren't being paid promptly. The problem, Guerrieri discovered, lay in the fact that the import department hadn't initially realized that the foreign brokers would be invoicing in their native languages, and expected to be paid in their native currencies. The accounts payable department had no personnel with the language skills necessary to translate the invoices, and had failed to realize the complications involved in making payments in foreign currencies.

Guerrieri met with representatives of the two departments, and began analysing the process. The first step was to define what the customer wanted. That was simple enough: the customers – the foreign brokers – wanted to be paid promptly in their own currency.

Guerrieri and the process improvement team then asked themselves the question: 'Where can the required language skills and access to foreign currencies be most easily found?' The answer was: in the IBM plants abroad that were producing the parts being imported into the USA! The solution then became obvious – the export brokers could invoice the IBM plants in their own countries, and those plants could then invoice IBM in the USA in dollars. Problem solved.

But that wasn't the end of it. Because the export brokers were now being paid so promptly, they were willing to reduce their fees: 'A difficult situation and complicated process was improved and streamlined into an efficient and cost-effective one,' Guerrieri says, 'by concentrating on the customer's requirements and how best to satisfy them.'

SUZIE LUPO'S STORY

Another tricky situation at IBM involved missing invoices. The accounts payable department was being blamed for this, and was determined to prove it wasn't guilty.

A team was formed to investigate the problem and find a solution. The team discovered that the 200 000 or more invoices that came in each month were sent to seven separate desks. Each member of the team was assigned a desk to investigate. Team members set up tracking sheets to follow invoices through the process. They discovered that there were a number of ways in which an invoice could go astray, according to Suzie Lupo:

> For example, people would send invoices, carbon copies and duplicate invoices all in the same package. They might tell us that they had sent us eight invoices, but only five of them might be actual invoices, the other three articles might be statements, or carbon copies, or duplicates of invoices we already had in the system.

The team met to discuss its findings, and then worked out solutions. They created new forms to track invoices. They created form letters to send to customers, explaining common invoicing errors, and a change in computer operations prevented duplicate electronic invoices from entering the system. The team also created a new report that catches duplicate payments before they are despatched, saving the company a million dollars a month.

The team approach to solving process problems has been so successful that it is being applied in other areas: 'Any time we want to solve a problem, we get a team together,' Lupo says. 'It's become a way of life here.'

PAUL CASEY'S LEADERSHIP PROFILE

IBM's Paul Casey also understands the value of process innovation, teams and Mind Maps, in particular the value of studying tasks at the granular level:

> By 'granular', I mean something that is at the very lowest level of a process. For example, in making a phone call, the steps are: first you think about it, then you look up the number, then you put your finger on the button of the phone, and so on. We trained people to think at a detailed level about what they were doing.

At a PITT Workshop, Casey notes that employees learned to work in a team environment:

> We then put action plans in place – specific action plans, names, dates, steps, places that we would use to put a fix in. And we even tracked savings from it. The savings were usually in terms

of hours. We generated a lot of savings because of the reduction of hours in particular processes. You can then take those hours and use them for whatever you want – reduction of overtime, freeing people up for other projects, freeing people up to do other parts of their job.

Casey reports that one particular change saved 93 hours a month:

Through the process work, we got people to think at a granular and very literal level about what they were doing – not to make assumptions about what they thought they were doing.

But Casey's words say more than might be apparent at first glance. They reflect the reality of what he has been doing by applying the Brain Principles and techniques that we've discussed in this book. He has been helping his employees tap the enormous potential of the human brain to become more effective, and to help create a more efficient, competitive company.

In short: 'We get people to think. Could a company – could a manager – ask for anything more?'

Casey was working with an accounting group within the company when he participated in a three-day PITT Workshop – a workshop that changed his organization.

Management wanted to find out where resources were *actually* being expended, rather than where the management team *thought* they were – this difference between perception and reality is called the 'Gap'. The results highlighted the need for process improvement and suggested some new directions for this 500-person organisation. Casey said:

We have experienced that all business can be helped by process analysis, but that such analysis is absolutely critical in organizations where there has been substantial personnel turnover, downsizing, changes in executive leadership, and changes in information systems, all of which were happening at IBM at the time.

Management wanted to avoid the common fad of 'business change through buzzwords'. Instead, we chose to teach people skills which they could use immediately on their jobs to solve problems that they were experiencing.

Two aspects of the programme particularly intrigued me. The first was being able to quantify dollar savings from specific process improvements. The second was learning a powerful tool – Mind Mapping.

During the workshop, participants worked on actual failures related to their jobs, using Mind Maps to help identify the root cause of those failures and possible solutions.

The workshop included five teams of five persons each. Some teams were composed of workers from only one department; others were made up of workers from several departments.

The accounting services function was split geographically. Bob Hughes, who was a peer manager from Endicott, and Paul Casey assumed the roles of advocates, administrators and teachers in training.

Casey's team's first problem was caused by incomplete data records that were transmitted to the payment system's database from many different sources. Each data record contained the sale price and product numbers from a specific sale. However, certain items were often missing. The defective records were either rejected from the automatic processsing routine or 'suspended'. The aggregate dollar amount due to each vendor was calculated accurately, but fixing the suspended records to arrive at the correct payment was very labour-intensive.

The team drew up a Mind Map starting with the 'suspend' report as its central image. They drew branches representing the input for IBM's geographical regions, the system used to process the data, the processing analysts, and the contract between IBM and the software vendor.

When the Mind Map was complete, it was obvious that the problem activity could be traced to one specific source. Now that the root cause of the problem was determined, a solution could be devised.

The solution involved working with programmers to develop a routine that would compare the data from the problem source with data containing information on installation dates, then modify the defective data as necessary. The net result was a great reduction in the staff time required for the comparison process.

The Mind Map allowed everyone to see the big picture. When the various components in the process were seen together, the failure point became obvious to everyone. The Mind Map in this instance was not complex, but it enabled the team to identify the problem immediately. Many other Mind Maps were subsequently used on other processes.

The workshop was intended to provide employees with new tools, improve process efficiency and cycle time, and help them learn to work as a team. It did all that and more. The number of worker-hours saved was measurable – and impressive. Resources could be managed more efficiently, and overtime decreased.

The workshops continued, and the programme has been expanded into other areas of the company. Casey said:

> I believe in the power of teams, Mind Maps, and Activity Analysis, because the results are irrefutable. These are powerful tools for employees in their jobs, careers, and even their personal lives.

Conclusion

The PITT Workshop helps teams solve a common problem in many organizations – focusing so much on the big picture that everyone loses sight of the details, or being lost in the details and not seeing the big picture.

Imagine the power generated by an organization which recognizes the uniqueness of each individual and has the capacity to focus them on common goals with the precision of a laser beam. Despite the discrete boxes in their organizational chart, every company is really a collection of individuals, each possessing personal strengths. To excel in today's business environment, an innovative company must harness the creative potential of all its employees in a way which aligns them with executive leadership.

ACTIVITIES

1a. List six activities that you perform as part of your current job. An activity must contain an action verb and an object noun so that the reader would clearly picture the physical action in which you are engaged. For example, an activity could be 'I am processing (action verb) a customer order (noun) into the scheduling system'.

1b. In looking at your activity list, note if there are any activities which are 50 per cent or more related to working on failures/corrections/errors.

2. Show your activity list to another person and ask them to describe back to you their understanding of your activities.

3. Meet with a customer (internal or external) on an activity and ask them how they use the output of the activity.

4. Take an activity from Exercise 1a and construct a Mind Map showing the reasons for any failure task that may exist within it.

5. List all the benefits you have realized from conducting the exercise to this stage.

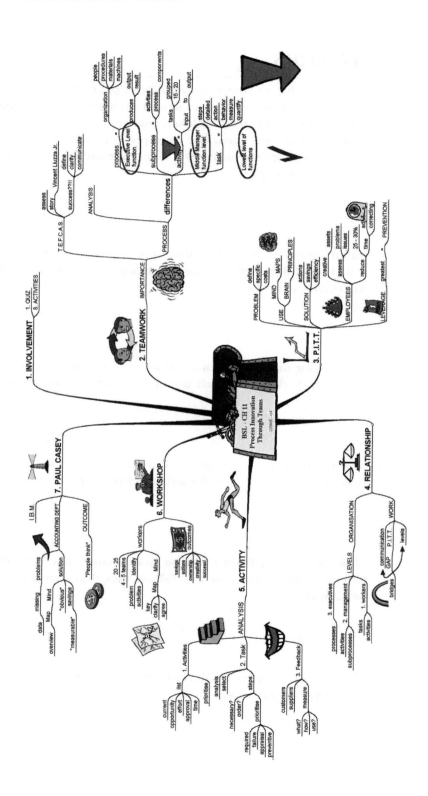

EPILOGUE: THE TONY ANGELO STORY

In 1996 Tony Angelo, current Project Executive for Worldwide Employee Disbursements at IBM, replaced Rich Bannon (profiled in Chapter 1). The foundation had already been laid to make the IBM Worldwide Employee Disbursements Accounting organization the best it had ever been. Angelo could see immediately how beneficial the implementation of the PITT Workshops had been in improving efficiency, and how it provided the groundwork to make continuous innovation the standard.

Soon after assuming his new role, Angelo realized that the organization was ready to move to the next level. Thanks to his predecessor, all the carefully crafted building blocks for a world-class organization were in place. It was now up to him to assemble them into a unified structure.

To build that structure, he has concentrated on identifying critical interfaces in work processes, analysis of redundancies, finding the most efficient way of sequencing and performing activities, and building communication channels throughout the whole process. Measurements are established at the critical interfaces, creating a key element of the management feedback system. It has provided the framework for Angelo's team to use the PITT tools even more effectively, and has led to dramatic improvements in process efficiencies.

As a result, Angelo's total spending has been reduced in each of the last two years, despite salary increases, higher bonus payouts to employees and an increase of more than a 20 per cent in processed transactions. Bannon's and Angelo's organizations were so effective that IBM won the prestigious Reach Award from *CFO Magazine* for re-engineering the travel accounting area in 1996. In 1997, IBM's Travel and Payroll department was a finalist for that same award due to process improvements of 20–50 per cent over their prior award-winning effort. It marked the first time that payroll processes were included as part of award selection criteria.

One vital aspect of the building process is requiring the key people in each organization to communicate with their counterparts in other organizations before they make policy. This ensures that no ripple effect from a proposed change will unintentionally damage any other part of the organization, or affect it without that organization's prior knowledge or consent.

For example, under the previous system, Human Resources might have decided to award deserving employees a non-monetary bonus, such as gift certificates from a catalogue. In the past, this change would simply have been announced without consulting those who were likely to find their workload increased because of it. The problem was, no one had considered what this seemingly good idea meant to the people working in Payroll. Without any say in the process, Payroll employees were now responsible for deciding how to apply appropriate taxes to these awards and report them as income. No matter how efficiently they resolved the new reporting requirements, it meant more work for their department. The Payroll department would become frustrated and angry that they had not been consulted before another department implemented a policy that would significantly increase their workload. Had their opinion been solicited, they might have persuaded Human Resources not to implement this particular programme, or they might have suggested ways to do it which still achieved the desired goals – to reward deserving employees – without causing unnecessary stress or expenditure for the the Payroll department.

'With the new system, I sit down with my counterparts in different areas at least quarterly, and ask them about their short- and long-term plans, and then we make decisions as a team,' explained Angelo. 'This way, we come up with the best and least expensive way to carry out our plans, and everyone who will be affected knows about the plans and has input as to how they are executed. What's important is deciding on the right overall solution for IBM, as opposed to what's best at an individual functional level.'

Angelo also developed another procedure to consolidate processes:

> We evolved to the point that we knew there were certain activities being done in one area, such as Travel, which were similar to what was being done in Relocation. We also realized that the same activites were performed differently by identical or very similar departments in different locations. We looked at all this and realized that there was no reason these processes couldn't all be the same.

He called together representatives from all the departments. Together, they created standardized ways to report their activities and communicate with Angelo and his staff. Thanks to this new system, he spends far less time deciphering reports and has a more accurate picture of what is going on in his entire organization.

Before determining what a new process should look like, he and his team spend a good deal of time analysing the systems in all the departments, extracting the best practices from each to make up the new standardized system. For example, Payroll is charged with collecting overpayments to employees. The International Assignee Payroll staff in Mt Pleasant, New York, had developed a series of standard collection letters which were effective and non-abrasive. However, these letters were generated manually, and were not tracked very efficiently. On the other hand, the Payroll staff in Endicott, New York, had automated its collections process, but sent out letters which annoyed recipients. Now, both Payroll departments send out letters combining the tone of those developed in Mt Pleasant and the efficient process of letter-generation and follow-up developed at Endicott.

Even more standardization and efficiency are on the way as Angelo and his teams formulate ways to use emerging technology. They foresee that in the not-too-distant future, employees who want to book a business trip will be able to log onto IBM's home page on the Internet, enter their requirements, such as where they are going, how long they are staying and which hotel they prefer, and the trip will be booked automatically, in compliance with the travel contracts and policy. They will also be given other pertinent information, such as maps, recommended restaurants, and security alerts. At the same time, the employee's manager will be notified of the travel arrangements and any policy exceptions booked by the employee.

When the employee returns, they will log back onto the terminal, where any expenses charged on the corporate credit card will already have been automatically entered in the appropriate blanks, greatly reducing the amount of time they must spend filing expenses. If these expenses are within corporate policy, the report won't have to go to the manager for approval. It will be analysed, and the credit card bill will be paid automatically. This reduces time spent by others in processing and auditing travel expense reports. This vision cannot be accomplished without cross-functional teamwork between people from the various sections of the organization: Human Resources, Procurement, IBM Travel Vendors, and Information Technology.

Despite the successes experienced in his various departments, Angelo is not resting on his laurels. His innovative management methods are IBM's leadership system of choice, he is currently upgrading payroll and travel systems around the globe, and the management team of Bill Lyons (National Payroll Services), Jim Fedorchak (Travel/Relocation), John Rosato (Change Management) and Jim Callahan (International Assignment Accounting) have been instrumental in deploying the PITT tools and techniques throughout Angelo's world-wide organization.

'I view what we do as dynamic as opposed to static,' he explained. 'We're continuing to streamline the process, to improve and to re-engineer. It's much easier to re-engineer something if you know in fairly good detail what your existing process looks like and how well it is performed. It's much easier to define improvement goals when you know where you are. That is one of the overriding factors. Also, it facilitates our selection of IT solutions.'

Tony Angelo's journey of success and continuing improvement is a prime example of how powerful the seven Brain Principles can be when all are implemented. He learned them during a PITT Workshop, and has used his knowledge of them to both identify ones he was already using and to implement others to make himself a BrainSmart Leader. Below are brief sketches of how he sees himself using the principles. When we first interviewed Angelo, he felt his organization had used only six of the seven.

Brain Principle 1: The brain synergizes information, so that 1 plus 1 is two or more

To tackle problems, generate solutions or formulate policy, Angelo often assembles teams of people drawn from diverse disciplines and departments. He finds that this 'cross-pollination' results in more creativity. An accountant, for example, may devise a good idea for one of the travel agents, or vice versa, despite their initial unfamiliarity with each other's work activities.

> The creativity that results from getting Human Resources, Information Technology, Procurement and Vendors together is just amazing. What we get is a much broader thinking style.

Brain Principle 2: The brain is a success-driven mechanism

'Every small success we've experienced has driven us to larger and larger successes. The successes compound as they build upon each other.'

Brain Principle 4: The brain craves completeness – it needs to fill in the blanks

'I have to see how all the pieces fit together. I look for end-to-end process definitions of work, including all the input and output of each activity. That's why I handle my departments as I do – to see the whole picture.'

Brain Principle 5: The brain constantly seeks new information and knowledge

'It is imperative with our use of technology that our people continue to learn, so we are constantly exposing them to training. It's the only way to stay on top of the game.'

Brain Principle 6: The brain is truth-seeking

'I insist on knowing the important facts. You can't deal with opinions when faced with a situation. To make the best decisions, you must focus on the right details, from process flows through metrics.'

Brain Principle 7: The brain is persistent

'I think those who know me will agree that I'm persistent. I will take "no" for an answer only when I've been given a thorough explanation and am convinced that a situation is the way I'm told it is. If I'm not sure someone is telling me the complete story, I keep pushing them until they do. I also have a very good memory for what others are supposed to do, and I won't give up until I know they have done it.'

Brain Principle 3: The brain has the ability to mimic actions perfectly

> At first, I was not sure that we used this principle. However, I realized that the concept of taking best practices from each area and duplicating them in all other areas used the mimic principle. I guess we *do* use all seven!

As Angelo reflects on his organization's successes, he is confident that with people sharing ideas, enthusiastic about what they do, and with leaders who understand how to build rapidly Intellectual Capital, his team will consistently find the best way to get the job done.

He summarizes it for us in the following message:

> Today, successful companies recognize that the only constant is 'change'. We established the foundation for us to create quickly, to adapt and implement changes to our processes. Our employees have a very powerful tool that allows them not only to cope with change, but to promote change. To lead the pack, you must innovate and get the job done better than anyone else. It's not rocket science. It's just a straightforward way of approaching leadership.

Conclusion

In this book, we have described some people we consider to be BrainSmart Leaders, the new agents of corporate change. Leaders who win respect, commitment, integrity and loyalty from their people. Leaders who cultivate and engage employee talents that are aligned and committed to their organizations' vision. Rich Bannon, Tony Angelo, Tiger Vessels, Tom Bering, Bob Hughes, Sandy Hahn, Jim Kalinowski, Candace Jones, Mary Vasso-Ortega and Bruce Wagner are just a few of the BrainSmart Leaders who will take us into the future.

As we saw with Tony Angelo, who took over the helm from Rich Bannon at IBM, the process continues growing in strength as Angelo develops his team for the long haul, building both professional and psychological stamina.

You too can achieve all this yourself. You now have the tools in your hands

– the techniques to develop an aligned workforce, focused on your company's goals, energized, self-motivated and showing constant improvements in the return on investments.

We wish you well on this exciting journey.

BrainSmart!

STOP PRESS

Both Tony Angelo and Bob Hughes have received the 1998 CFO (Chief Financial Officer) Magazine Reach Awards honouring outstanding achievement in financial process and re-engineering for Employee Processing and Vendor Processing. This is the highest form of official recognition that these BrainSmart Leaders can achieve.

FURTHER READING

Buzan, T with Buzan, B (1995), *The Mind Map Book: Radiant Thinking*, London: BBC Books

Buzan, T (1995), *Use Your Head*, London: BBC Books

Buzan, T (1995), *Use Your Memory*, London: BBC Books

Buzan, T (1997), *The Speed Reading Book*, London: BBC Books

North, V with Buzan, T (1996), *Get Ahead*, Poole: BBC Books

Buzan, T with Keene, R (1996), *The Age Heresy*, London: Ebury Press

Buzan, T and Keene, R (1994), *Buzan Book of Genius*, London: Stanley Paul

Buzan, T and Israel, R (1995), *Brain Sell*, Aldershot: Gower

Buzan, T and Israel, R (1997), *SuperSellf*, Aldershot: Gower

Israel, R and Crane, J (1996), *The Vision*, Aldershot: Gower

Buzan, T and Israel, R (1999), *Sales Genius*, Aldershot: Gower

TO CONTACT THE AUTHORS

Tony Buzan
c/o Buzan Centres Ltd
54 Parkstone Road
Poole
Dorset BH15 2PG
England
Tel: 44 (0) 1202 674676
Fax: 44 (0) 1202 674776
Email: Buzan@Mind-Map.com
Website: www.Mind-Map.com

Tony Dottino
14 Lafayette Road
Larchmont
NY 10538
USA
Tel: 1 (201) 666–5804
Fax: 1 (201) 666–2728
Email: Adottino@aol.com
Website: www.qsilvertlc.com

Richard Israel
900 NE 195th Street, Suite 606
Miami
FL 33179
USA
Tel: 1 (305) 655–2675
Fax: 1 (305) 770–0926
Email: Brainsell@aol.com
Website: www.qsilvertlc.com

RESOURCES

For all information concerning Buzan Mental Literacy courses and products, please contact:

in North America
Buzan Centres Inc.
415 Federal Highway
Lake Park
FL 33403
USA
Tel: 1-800Y-MINDMAP or 1 (516) 881 0188
Fax: 1 (516) 845 3210
Email: Buzan000@aol.com
Website: www.Mind-Map.com

in Europe
Buzan Centres Ltd
54 Parkstone Road
Poole
Dorset BH15 2PG
England
Tel: 44 (0) 1202 674676
Fax: 44 (0) 1202 674776
Email: Buzan@Mind-Map.com
Website: www.Mind-Map.com

For information about BrainSmart Leadership workshops, contact the authors.

For information about PITT workshops, contact Tony Dottino.

INDEX